Hippocrene Great Religions of the World
THE EPISCOPAL CHURCH

Hippocrene Great Religions of the World
THE EPISCOPAL CHURCH

David Locke

HIPPOCRENE BOOKS
New York

For information, contact:
HIPPOCRENE BOOKS, INC.
171 Madison Avenue
New York, NY 10016

Library of Congress Cataloging-in-Publication Data available.

ISBN 0-87052-900-5

Printed in the United States of America

Contents

Introduction

THE EPISCOPAL CHURCH IS AN AMERICAN CHRISTIAN church which has its roots in the Church of England. Officially known as the Protestant Episcopal Church in the United States of America, it was formed by English colonists, ministers and laymen, who came to America in the 150 years before the Revolution. It separated from the English church shortly after the war. The Episcopal church is a member of the Anglican Communion, a group of nearly thirty national churches around the world, all with similar ties to the Church of England.

Although the Episcopal church is most properly classed as a Protestant church, like other churches in the Anglican Communion it is both Catholic and Protestant. It is Catholic in the sense that it is derived from the early universal Christian church. In fact, the word *Episcopal* refers to the fact that the church has bishops who extend back in a direct line to the Apostles. Yet, the church is Protestant because it does not recognize the authority of the pope and has accepted many of the reforms introduced during the Protestant Reformation.

Inasmuch as the Episcopal church has elements in common with the Roman Catholic and Protestant churches, it is sometimes referred to as a bridge church, or as the *via media*, a Latin phrase meaning the middle way. It also has kinship with the Eastern Orthodox churches which have bishops but are not aligned with the Roman Catholic church. Through its relationships with other churches, the Episcopal church has long been involved in the ecumenical movement, an effort to bring about cooperation, ultimately unity, among the churches.

There is sometimes tension between those in the church who emphasize one aspect, Protestant or Catholic, over the other. Those who prefer to see the church as Protestant are generally referred to as low church, and those who favor the Catholic element are called high church. Many others do not like these distinctions and speak of themselves as being broad church. Most of the time, these groups reconcile their differences and work together amicably.

The Episcopal church is not large. It has some two-and-a-half million members in the United States (compared to the Roman Catholic church's forty million). But it is influential, partly because of its character as a bridge church and partly because it has had a disproportionate share of historically important figures as members. The bulk of the founding fathers belonged to the church, as were five of the first thirteen chief justices of the Supreme Court. Twelve presidents of the United States, including George Washington and George Bush, have been Episcopalians, more than have belonged to any other single denomination.

In Congress, too, Episcopalians often held a disproportionate share of the seats. Although they constituted little more than one percent of the U.S. population in 1989, Episcopalians held 12 percent of the seats in the

House of Representatives during the 101st Congress. And in the Senate that year, Episcopalians occupied 20 percent of the seats, more than any other denomination. As might be expected, the church's National Cathedral in Washington, D.C., the seat of its presiding bishop, plays an important part in the life of the nation's capital.

Later chapters of this book will look at the church and the Anglican communion in more detail. But in order to understand properly what the Episcopal church is like, and to appreciate the special features of Anglicanism, one must see how the Anglican churches have come to be the kind of churches they are. To do this, one must begin at the beginning, and that is not in America but in Britain, sometime in the first centuries after the birth of Christ.

PART ONE

THE CHURCH OF ENGLAND

I

Founding the Church of England

THE CHRISTIAN CHURCH REACHED THE BRITISH ISLES VERY early, with the Roman legions. Many of the Roman soldiers were Christians. The exact date of the arrival of the church cannot be determined, but it was probably in the first or second century, for history records that two bishops from England attended a church council at Arles, in France, in the year 314.

In the fourth and fifth centuries the authority of Rome weakened, and the descendants of the Romans in Britain gradually merged with the native Celts, whom they had influenced and made Christians. When Anglo-Saxon invaders later poured into Britain from Northern Europe, they drove the Celts into the west of England, and Wales. There, for three centuries, a Celtic

Christian church flourished, producing illuminated manuscripts and religious art works of great beauty. The famous St. Patrick traveled as a missionary from Britain to Ireland in the fifth century, and St. Columba went to Scotland in the sixth. During this period the austere, monastic Celts were virtually the only active Christians in northwestern Europe.

In 597 Pope Gregory (the "Great") sent to Anglo-Saxon Britain a missionary team headed by St. Augustine (a monk from the monastery of St. Andrew, in Rome, not the earlier and better-known Bishop of Hippo, in North Africa). Greatly impressed by St. Augustine, as well as by Celtic missionaries, the Anglo-Saxons were rapidly converted to Christianity. The Celtic and Roman churches had developed separate practices, including different dates for the celebration of Easter, and this caused some confusion in the newly formed Anglo-Saxon church. In 664, however, a synod of the church finally decided to accept the Roman usages.

It was the strong and vigorous Anglo-Saxon church of the eighth century that produced the noted scholar St. Bede (the "Venerable"), and made other important contributions to learning. Also at this time, the English church was divided into two provinces, headed respectively by the archbishop of Canterbury, a post first held by St. Augustine, and a newly created archbishop of York. This division persists. (Confusingly, the archbishop of York is titled "primate of England," while the archbishop of Canterbury is "primate of all England.")

With the Norman conquest of England in 1066, a new element was added to the English church. Along with his Norman court, William the Conqueror brought with him Norman clergymen, including an Italian named Lanfranc, whom he made archbishop of Canterbury. As archbishop, Lanfranc supported the efforts of the new pope Gregory VII to reform the church and bring it firmly under the control of Rome. He held local synods, asserted the primacy of the see of Canterbury, and introduced Roman canon law into England. Also at this time, the Cistercian order of monks made their way to England from France.

While William was content to see the centralization of authority within the English church, he resisted all efforts of Pope Gregory to assert the power of the papacy over his kingdom. He refused to swear fealty to the pope—though he sent him money—and he forbade communication between the papacy and the English church without his consent. He himself remained head of the church courts as well as the civil ones.

With the addition of Norman influences, the character of the English church was set in a pattern that prevailed for some 500 years. From its Celtic roots the church inherited a spirit of devotion and a tradition of mysticism. From its Anglo-Saxon forebears it gained an earnest simplicity, strength, and vigor. And from the Norman newcomers it acquired a love of beauty, grandeur, and ceremony. The flourishing English church now took its place among the great medieval churches of Europe.

It was a Christian age in England. The Cistercian monks were followed by Cluniacs, Carthusians, and those of many smaller orders. Great cathedrals and monasteries were built across the land, the Romanesque giving way to the Gothic style. Universities were established in Oxford and Cambridge and clerical learning blossomed. The most famous scholars from the church were Roger Bacon, Robert Grosseteste, and William of Ockham. Englishmen fought in the crusades. There were English saints, among them William and Hugh. There was even an English pope, Adrian IV.

As with many of the churches of the Middle Ages, the loyalties of the English church were divided between king and pope. Much of the difficulty centered on the archbishop of Canterbury, an appointee of the king but also a legate, or delegate, of the pope. In the most dramatic, and tragic, instance, Archbishop Thomas à Becket was murdered at the indirect suggestion of King Henry II. Most English kings, like William the Conqueror, succeeded in maintaining their independence from Rome, but Henry's son, King John, was forced to surrender his crown to the pope and formally held his kingdom in fief to Rome.

The conflict between church and state came to a head during the reign of the Tudor king, Henry VIII, from 1509 to 1547. It is sometimes said, by those unsympathetic to the Church of England, that it was founded by Henry VIII to secure a divorce for the purpose of marrying Anne Boleyn, a lady of the court. The matter is more complicated than this.

There can be little doubt that Henry was motivated chiefly by a desire to leave a male heir to the throne. He had been married early in life to his elder brother's widow, the Spanish princess Catherine of Aragon. Catherine had borne Henry a daughter, Mary, but they had no other surviving children. Henry took, or claimed to take, this as God's judgment on the legitimacy of his marriage, which was contrary to canon law and had only been made possible by a dispensation from the pope. Now Henry sought to have the pope annul the marriage so he might remarry and produce a male heir.

Pope Clement VII did not refuse outright, and apparently did not oppose Henry on religious grounds. Nevertheless, he was prevented from acting by Catherine's nephew, the Holy Roman Emperor, Charles V, who feared that a new marriage might make Henry an ally of France. After some years of this impasse, Henry resolved the matter by declaring himself "supreme head" of the church in England. He then proceeded to void his own marriage and marry Anne Boleyn, whom he had come to love.

It is likely that Henry believed that he was not exerting any greater authority over the English church than had earlier English kings, and it was not his intent to separate the English church completely from the rest of the Catholic church. Initially, certainly, he did not join the Protestant Reformation, which had been started by Martin Luther in 1517. In fact, Henry's earlier opposition to Luther had inspired the pope to hail him as Defender of the Faith.

Henry's actions found considerable support among the English people. Not unanimous support, however. Henry's own lord chancellor, the learned Thomas More, became a martyr for refusing to acknowledge the king's supremacy over the church. But there was much anticlerical sentiment in England. The English church, like the church on the Continent, had grown fat, complacent, corrupt, and powerful. It was much resented.

More than a century before, the reformer John Wycliffe had repeatedly denounced the corruption of the clergy. Now Henry found his country largely behind him when he moved to take over the church. His dissolution of the monasteries and appropriation of their assets for the Crown met with favor from the common people.

Though Henry still thought of himself and his church as Catholic, many of those who applauded his efforts were in sympathy with Martin Luther and the Protestant revolution. The archbishop of Canterbury, Thomas Cranmer, supported Lutheran ideas. Furthermore, Henry had frequent dealings with the Lutheran powers of Northern Europe, and for political reasons, he tolerated the spread of Lutheran belief in his kingdom. Yet, by the end of Henry's reign, the practices of his church had barely changed. The English church had acquired a tinge of Protestantism and had broken from the pope, but it remained essentially Catholic.

That tinge of Protestantism grew under the reign of Henry's son, Edward VI (born of Henry's third wife, Jane Seymour). Edward was nine when he came to the throne in 1547. He was a sickly, intellectual lad, and his office was actually exercised by his uncle, the Duke of Somerset, as regent. The young king was also much influenced by Archbishop Cranmer. Thus the powers behind the throne were all staunchly Protestant, mostly followers of John Calvin, the Swiss reformer, rather than the German Luther.

During Edward's reign, an austere form of Calvinism took over the English church. Statues were banished from churches. Altars were demolished and holy tables set up in their place. The clergy set aside their elaborate vestments and wore simple black gowns.

But the most far-reaching development of the period was Archbishop Cranmer's introduction of an English prayerbook. Since Henry's day it had become customary to read the Bible in English rather than Latin, and several English prayers were introduced into services. Now Thomas Cranmer produced a complete book of English prayers, in two, successively more Protestant versions, those of 1549 and 1552. Because Archbishop Cranmer was something of a conservative, even as he was a Protestant, his prayerbook laid out a form of worship that incorporated both Catholic and Protestant ideals. He also had an extraordinary gift for using the English language in dramatic and moving forms—so extraordinary that his prayerbook served the church well for more than four centuries.

With Edward's untimely death in 1553, the throne passed to his elder sister Mary, daughter of Catherine of Aragon. Thirty-seven years old when she came to the throne, and considered illegitimate after Henry had annulled his marriage to her mother, Mary was determined to restore Roman Catholicism to England. She insisted on marrying the Catholic king, Phillip II of Spain, eleven years her junior. The marriage found almost no support in England.

Even more unpopular were the steps Mary took to return the English church to the papal fold. To begin with, she restored the Latin Mass. Then she removed many of the reforming bishops and priests, especially those who had committed the sin of matrimony. Within a year the pope welcomed England home. But England was not happy to be there. The confirmed Protestants among Mary's subjects could not follow her lead. In particular, they objected to the newly proclaimed Roman doctrine of transubstantiation, the belief that the substance of the bread and wine was physically changed to the body and blood of Christ during the celebration of the Mass.

What Mary could not accomplish by fiat, she determined to do by fear. She began to burn Protestant heretics at the stake, including Thomas Cranmer. The archbishop had sworn to follow his sovereign in religious matters. He had done so with Henry and Edward, and also tried with Mary, even going beyond the limits of his conscience. At her demand, he signed one humiliating recantation after another. But as he was taken to be burned, he denounced them all and, with them, the pope. In four years Mary ordered the deaths of three hundred persons, men and women, bishops, priests, and laymen. The burning stopped only with her own death. It was these actions which ensured that Mary, ever after, would be known to the English people as Bloody Mary. Mary Tudor had sought to make the English nation Roman Catholic. She ensured that it never again would be.

The Tudor sovereigns of England were stubborn and determined. Even young Edward was willful, and probably would have made a strong king. But two of them also understood the English people and knew how to win their hearts. Henry had done so with skill; and Mary's half-sister and successor, Elizabeth, daughter of Anne Boleyn, did so consummately.

One of the first things Elizabeth did was restore to

the English people their church—not the church of
Edward, but that of Henry. Both Catholic and Protestant, but neither Roman Catholic nor austerely Calvinist, it was thoroughly English. Elizabeth reinstated
the 1552 version of Thomas Cranmer's English prayerbook with some modifications to render it acceptable to
the more Catholic of her subjects. She then assumed
the title "supreme governor" instead of "supreme head"
of the church, a change that was meant to emphasize
that she held temporal, not spiritual, authority over the
church.

Elizabeth appointed bishops judiciously. She pla-
cated Protestants who had returned from abroad after
Mary's oppression, but she did not turn the church over
to them. She did not acknowledge the supremacy of the
pope, but she was content to have loyal Roman Catholics remain in the English church until the pope condemned her as a heretic and excommunicated her,
along with all who followed her.

Finally, she supervised the preparation of the Thirty-
nine Articles that established the official doctrine of
the church. They differed appreciably from the Ten
Articles, quite Catholic, that had been proclaimed by
Henry, and the Forty-two Articles, strongly Calvinist,
announced under Edward. So carefully were the various influences balanced in the Thirty-nine Articles that
they can be interpreted as both Catholic and Calvinist,
and they remain to this day the official statement of
church doctrine.

From its Celtic, Anglo-Saxon, and Norman roots, the
English church drew its essential inner nature. In Elizabeth's reign the church acquired the outer aspect that
has marked it to the present time. It was still Catholic,

and proud that its bishops followed in unbroken line through the early Catholic church back to the Apostles. But it was separate and distinct from the Roman Catholic church, and after the experience with Mary Tudor, somewhat antagonistic to it. It was strongly influenced by the Protestant churches in ritual and belief, but held back from breaking completely with the past. Above all, it was devoted to its own English prayers and prayerbook.

II

The English Church Tested

BY THE END OF THE SIXTEENTH CENTURY, THE CHURCH OF England was firmly set on its course as a national church, in effect both Catholic and Protestant. The seventeenth and eighteenth centuries saw the church sorely tried, but ultimately strengthened.

Elizabeth's successor to the English throne in 1603 was the Scottish king James VI (James I of England), son of Elizabeth's old rival, Mary, Queen of Scots. James had been raised among the Scottish Presbyterians and had no liking for them; in England he strongly supported the bishops and threw his weight behind the most Catholic party within the church. In opposition to James, the more extreme Protestants, known as Puritans, grew strong. They were popular, and well represented in Parliament, which became increasingly unsympathetic towards the king.

Yet, James' reign was not without its churchly glories. As head of the church, he commissioned a new English translation of the Bible, and the resulting Authorized, or King James Version was so successful that for more than three centuries it has been *the* Bible of the English-speaking world. The English church, more than any other, makes regular Bible-reading part of its service, and wherever Englishmen have gone, the King James Version has gone with them. Its words, its voice, have become the bedrock of the English language. For centuries English-speaking people who knew no other book, knew this one, thoroughly. Thus, to Thomas Cranmer's prayerbook, and Queen Elizabeth's Thirty-nine Articles, King James added the English Bible to complete the seminal writings of the English church.

The seveteenth century was a time when people took their religion seriously. Among the well-known preachers of the day was Lancelot Andrewes, bishop of Chichester, Ely, and Winchester, who left behind a memorable book of devotions. Perhaps the greatest preacher of the time was a Roman Catholic convert, John Donne, who today is chiefly noted for his powerful devotional poetry.

James' son, Charles I, succeeded him in 1625 and proved himself unable to control the ill-feeling that his father had unleashed among Puritans, Parliament, and the English people. His choice for archbishop of Canterbury, William Laud, came from the most Catholic wing of the church and was unjustly suspected of being in sympathy with the Roman Catholics. Between them,

Charles and his archbishop infuriated the Puritans and Parliament with their high-handed behavior, and in 1642 the country erupted in civil war. After seven years of bloody strife, Parliament prevailed. King and archbishop lost their heads.

The execution of the king ended what came to be called the Great Rebellion. In 1649 England was declared a commonwealth, with Oliver Cromwell, leader of the parliamentary armies, named lord protector somewhat later. Presbyterianism was now the official religion of England, and the Puritans reigned supreme. Bishops were deposed, and vacant seats left unfilled, until only nine bishops remained in all of England and Wales. It began to seem as though the apostolic succession—the direct line of bishops consecrated by other bishops leading back to the Twelve Apostles—would finally be broken in England. In all, some 3,600 ministers unsympathetic to the new rulers were dismissed. The starkest form of Puritanism was now the rule, and was strictly enforced. The prayerbook was outlawed, and even the mild festivities that traditionally took place on Sundays and at Christmas were forbidden.

As Bloody Mary had made the English hate the Roman Catholics, so the Commonwealth made them fear and resent the Puritans. Hence, the restoration of Charles' son as King Charles II in 1660, and the return of the Anglican church were both warmly welcomed. Charles II determined that the church would now follow a moderate course. The prayerbook was slightly revised and then reintroduced. It now proved acceptable to all but the most extreme Protestants. Ministers appointed during the Commonwealth, however, were required to be ordained again by the restored bishops.

Unhappy over both measures, some Presybterians left the church.

Surprisingly perhaps, during the lengthy turmoil of the Commonwealth and the Restoration, a group of English theologians thrived at the University of Cambridge. Known as the Cambridge Platonists, they strove to unite the best philosophical speculation of the day with their Anglican beliefs. They resisted both Calvinists and high churchmen and insisted that Christians should be free to choose their own form of worship.

The accession of Charles II's brother to the throne, as James II, brought new troubles to the church. An avowed Roman Catholic, James initially worked well with the Anglicans. Soon, however, he began to seek better treatment for Catholics, as well as for Protestant Dissenters. The Declaration of Indulgence with which he aimed to accomplish this was challenged by seven bishops, including the archbishop of Canterbury. When the king responded by trying them for libel, they were found innocent—to great public rejoicing.

The suspicion that James intended to convert the country to Roman Catholicism was now widespread. When the queen gave birth to a male heir, who would presumably be raised a Catholic, matters came to a head. James had two daughters by an earlier marriage, both Protestants. The elder, Mary, was married to William of Orange, a powerful Calvinist military leader from the Netherlands. In 1688, with almost unanimous popular support, William and Mary were invited to rule England jointly. James fled the country at the appearance of William's army, and Parliament declared that he had abdicated. This so-called Glorious Revolution was accomplished without bloodshed.

Under William and Mary, the English church was determinedly Protestant. By law, the sovereign now had to be a member of the Church of England. Thus, the situation under James II could never recur. Furthermore, the Toleration Act of 1689 established the right of the Nonconformist Protestants—those who would not accept bishops and the prayerbook—to worship as they pleased. This act acknowledged for the first time that a Protestant minority could exist in England outside the established, or state, church. Since the time of Edward, control of the church had swung back and forth between high church Anglicans and Puritan reformers, but the church itself had been perceived as one body— the struggle was over who would dominate it. Now the church was in the hands of a broadly tolerant, or Latitudinarian, faction, but many of the extreme Puritans, Dissenters, were no longer part of it.

Defection also occurred at the other extreme when the archbishop of Canterbury and a small band of bishops decided that they could not, in conscience, foreswear their oath of allegiance to James and take a new one to William. For more than a century these Nonjurors maintained their own church in schism from the established church.

The eighteenth century in England was as calm politically as the seventeenth had been turbulent. It began with the accession of Mary's sister, Anne. After Anne's death in 1714, the throne passed to a German Protestant branch of the family, the electors of Hanover. The reigns of the Hanoverian kings George I, II, and III spanned the century. James II's reign had shown that no English sovereign could rule without Parliament, and the eighteenth century saw the development of true parliamentary government in Britain. Two strong political parties evolved, the Tories, or conservatives, and the Whigs, or liberals. They fought to command majorities in Parliament and thus provide the ministers of the Crown, the real governors of the country.

The church also now entered on more placid times. An established church could not help becoming bound up with national politics, but as the century proceeded, comfortable churchmen could be accused of taking little interest in either politics or religion.

Queen Anne was a high church Anglican, who personally favored the Tories. She supported the high church group by preventing Nonconformists from taking part in the Anglican sacrament of Holy Communion, or the Lord's Supper. During Anne's reign, disputes in the Convocations of Clergy, which met along with Parliament to deal with church affairs, were so acrimonious that the Convocations were called to meet only one more time in the next 150 years. One sign of the times was an attempt by the Whig government to remove from office the popular churchman Dr. Sacheverell. After a lengthy trial, Dr. Sacheverell was found guilty but received a very light sentence, and the Whig government itself fell. During her reign, Queen Anne made over certain Crown income to the church for charity. Ever since this has been known as Queen Anne's bounty.

Under the Hanoverian kings, the calm surface of religious life hid considerable ferment. One area of

tension stemmed from political and religious differences between the bishops and other clergy. The
bishops, appointed by a government that was mainly
Whig during this period, were themselves liberal and
low church, or Latitudinarian. The parochial clergy,
however, often selected by Tory landowners, tended to
be conservative high churchmen, many of whom opposed the Whig government and even, secretly, the
Protestant Hanoverian dynasty.

It was a time of great apparent strength for the established church. The old Nonjurors were dying off, and
the numbers of Roman Catholics and Dissenters remained small. But it was not, in fact, a religious time.
Even the clergy were widely influenced by deistic phi-
losophy, which taught the existence of God on the basis
of reason and evidence from the natural world, rather
than from the Bible.

Indeed, there was much complacency and some indifference to religion among the clergy, as among the
laymen. Many of the parochial clergy were poorly educated and trained. Some held livings at several parishes
and had so many responsibilities that they could not
fulfill them adequately. Many were farmers, hunters,
and club members, indistinguishable from the local
gentry. They were resistant to political change and sus-
picious of religious fervor.

Of course, there were learned and sincere clergy, too.
One of the most remarkable religious books of the century was *The Analogy of Religion,* an argument against
deism written in 1736 by Joseph Butler, the future
bishop of Bristol and Durham. Early in the century
Thomas Bray had founded the Society for Promoting
Christian Knowledge, to provide Bibles and libraries

for at home and in the colonies. He also organized the Society for the Propagation of the Gospel, which provided missionaries, chiefly for the American colonies.

Perhaps the most impressive preacher of the age was John Wesley. Together with his brother, Charles, a hymn writer, he traveled the country delivering compelling sermons and founding so-called Methodist Societies, which practiced a systematic method of religious study and devotion. Although the Wesley brothers were both ordained in the Anglican church and considered themselves members all their lives, their Methodism found little support from regular Anglicans. Following John Wesley's death in 1791, his many Methodist converts began a slow process of separation from the Church of England. Yet Wesley's thought would have considerable influence on the church in the next century.

III

The English Church Renewed

DURING THE NINETEENTH CENTURY THE CHURCH OF EN-
gland was invigorated by the actions of both its
Protestant and its Catholic wings. The century also
witnessed the spread of the church's influence around
the world, with the formation of the group of national
churches that together make up the Anglican Communion.

The nineteenth century began with considerable
pressure from the more Protestant clerical faction.
These clergymen styled themselves Evangelicals,
meaning that their chief concern was preaching and
spreading the gospel. A number of Evangelicals had left
the church as Methodists, but many remained as a
powerful force within the church. They worked not

21

only to spread the gospel but also to increase the church's efforts to aid the poor and the lower classes.

Perhaps the most significant Evangelical clergyman was Charles Simeon, fellow of King's College and vicar of Holy Trinity Church, Cambridge. Also extremely influential was the so-called Clapham Sect, a group of devoted Evangelical laymen, members of the congregation of the parish church in Clapham. Several of the group were active members of Parliament, where they worked for the aboliton of the slave trade and a number of political and social reforms. They were active in the establishment of the Church Missionary Society and the Religious Tract Society. Their quarterly publication, *The Christian Observer*, was widely read, and they supported Hannah More, the writer and philanthropist, in the development of Sunday schools for the children of the poor.

Not all the reformers of the day were Evangelicals. A notable exception was Dr. Thomas Arnold, headmaster of Rugby School. Dr. Arnold hoped to see a new, liberal church, which would pull together all dissenting groups and become, as the Church of England had once been, a truly national church.

There was considerable reform within the church, especially once King George IV succeeded his father in 1820. Greater religious toleration of Catholics and dissenting Protestants was sanctioned by Parliament in 1828 and 1829. The ancient Convocations were revived in 1852 to assist in church government. Later in the century, lay houses were added to the Convocations, though they did not receive legal status until 1919. Parliament also began to administer funds for impoverished clergy and established an Ecclesiastical Commission to correct some of the injustices in the stipends of the various clergy, and put the financial affairs of the church on a more businesslike basis.

If the first decades of the nineteenth century saw a rise in the influence of the Protestant wing of the church, the next decades felt the impact of the high church group. The Evangelicals had been concerned about carrying the gospel abroad and to the poor at home, but they did not give much thought to the sacred nature of the church, nor were they strong in church learning, particularly the early history of the church. These were hallmarks of the high church Oxford Movement, which dominated church thought for several decades from 1833.

The movement began with a sermon, "National Apostasy," delivered by John Keble, professor of poetry at Oxford and author of a volume of poems, *The Christian Year*, which was one of the most popular religious books of the age. In his sermon Keble strongly protested Parliament's reduction of the number of bishops in Ireland. His concern was not with the action itself but with the fact that it was carried out by Parliament which thus presumed to direct God's church in its labors.

Keble was soon joined by a number of like-minded Oxford men, including John Henry Newman, fellow of Oriel College and vicar of St. Mary's Church. The group published their views in pamphlets or tracts—they were often referred to as Tractarians—which were distributed to the clergy of England.

The Oxford Movement taught that the church was

primarily an instrument of God, only secondarily an arm of the state. They emphasized the apostolic succession and considered the Church of England a direct descendant of the early apostolic church. They popularized the phrase *via media*. Although they distrusted the Roman Catholic church and felt it had departed from the true path, they considered the Anglican church truly Catholic and referred to themselves as Anglo-Catholics. At the same time, they believed that the Protestant Reformation had been a mistake and deplored its influence on the English church. Indeed, they hoped to restore what they believed to be the practices of the early church—frequent celebration of Holy Communion, use of elaborate vestments and ceremonials, and a monastic style of life.

The tracts were terminated in 1841 with Newman's *Tract 90*, in which he sought to reconcile the Thirtynine Articles with the teachings of the Catholic church. Many of his readers took this to mean the Roman Catholic church, and the reaction was violent. Newman's ambivalent feelings did finally take him into the Roman Catholic fold in 1845, and he died in 1890, a cardinal.

Like Newman, many other members of the Oxford Movement became Roman Catholics when they felt their own church unsympathetic to them. Others, like Keble and Dr. Pusey, professor of Hebrew at Oxford and another early leader of the movement, remained Anglican.

In spite of understandable suspicion of "papist" influence, the Oxford Movement had a number of permanent effects on the church: the formation of religious orders, the founding of theological schools, an appreciation of the apostolic church and the church fathers, an emphasis on the sacramental nature of the Communion service, and an awareness of the importance of the ceremonial. If the Evangelicals had made the Anglican minister a preacher of the gospel, the Oxford Movement transformed him into the celebrant of a sacrament.

Although the departure of Newman and his followers shook the church, the ultimate effect of the Oxford Movement was to strengthen it. If nothing else, it undermined the casual indifference of much of the clergy and laity and demanded that the church be taken seriously once more.

In 1837 Queen Victoria came to the throne of England at the age of eighteen; she would reign until 1901. During this period, the country underwent more momentous change than in any other single reign since that of Elizabeth. When Victoria came to the throne, the industrial revolution was just beginning. By the time of her death, the country had become a manufacturing and trading center for the world. The technological and social changes heralded by the railroad, the telegraph, the steam engine, and the gas light brought England from the world of Shakespeare to the world of our grandparents.

And political empire followed in the wake of commerce. The loss of the American colonies severely reduced England's possessions overseas. But over the next century new dominions were added in North America, Australia, Africa, and even India, where Victoria was named empress in 1876. From 1884 to 1902, two and one half million square miles were brought under the sway of the Crown.

Under Victoria, the church was also transformed. The day of the kindly but bumbling country parson, and the bishop nodding and dozing in the House of Lords, was to be no more. The missionary movement begun by the Evangelicals prompted the growth of foreign missions which ultimately spawned the series of independent, national churches that comprise the Anglican Communion today.

The formation of new churches began close to home. In Scotland, Presbyterianism had mostly prevailed since the Reformation, but there were periods in which bishops had been imposed by English monarchs, despite popular sentiment. In 1690 William and Mary acknowledged Presbyterianism as the official religion of Scotland. As a result, the remaining Scottish bishops—called Nonjurors like the English bishops who refused to acknowledge William and Mary—established their own Episcopal church in Scotland. In 1811 a national synod of that church accepted the Thirty-nine Articles, and ever since the Scottish Episcopal church has had friendly relations with the Church of England.

Unlike the Scots, the Irish remained essentially Roman Catholic throughout the Reformation. Under Queen Elizabeth, the Church of England was established as the official church, but it remained largely the church of the English gentry, unaccepted by the native Irish. In 1871 the Church of Ireland was finally disestablished and became like the Scottish church, a minority church in communion with the Church of England.

Probably because Wales had long been more closely tied with England than either Scotland or Ireland, the church in Wales did not receive independent status until 1920. Since much of the Welsh population is Methodist, it too is a minority church.

Following the Revolution, Anglicans in America saw the need for their own bishops. The first of these, Samuel Seabury, was actually consecrated in 1784 in Aberdeen, Scotland, by three nonjuring bishops. This is the beginning of the story of the Episcopal church in America, to which we will soon turn.

The flood of American loyalists into Canada after the Revolution vastly enlarged the church there. The first bishop of Nova Scotia was consecrated in 1787, and a bishop of Quebec was named in 1793. The first province of Canada was created in 1862, and the first General Synod of the Anglican Church of Canada was held in 1893.

Missionary work began early in India, and the first bishop of Calcutta was consecrated in 1813, with all of India and Australia as his diocese. Other bishops were subsequently appointed in India, but the separate Church of India, Pakistan, Burma, and Ceylon did not come into existence until 1930.

The first Australian bishop was named in 1836, and one for New Zealand, five years later. A constitution for the New Zealand church was signed in 1857; the General Synod of Australia was formed in 1872. The first Provincial Synod of the bishops of the province of South Africa had already met in 1861. As the century progressed, the groundwork for independent churches was laid in other parts of Africa, and in the West Indies, South America, China, and Japan.

While the English church was spreading abroad in the nineteenth century, it was also experiencing great domestic change. In addition to the revival of the Convocations and the administrative reforms already described, Diocesan Conferences and Church Congresses were held. New dioceses were created in Manchester, Ripon, St. Albans, Truro, Liverpool, Newcastle, Southwell, and Wakefield. Assistant, or suffragan, bishops were appointed to make church government more effective.

At the same time, the church's role in lay education was greatly diminished. Both Oxford and Cambridge universities were largely freed from religious control and discrimination. New, strictly secular—non-religious—colleges were founded, and state schools assumed responsibility for educating the young at all levels.

In fact, the latter part of the Victorian period was something of a secular age, especially among intellectuals. Darwin's theory of evolution, which seemed to deny the teachings of Genesis, was but part of a wider pattern of doubt, or agnosticism, and real disbelief, or atheism. The poet and critic Matthew Arnold, and the scientist Thomas Henry Huxley, were prominent agnostics, if not atheists. Within the church two books created an enormous furor: *Essays and Reviews*, an attempt by a number of young churchmen to deal with the Bible in a modern and critical way; and *Ecce Homo*

(Behold the Man), a biography of Jesus by Sir John Seeley, which emphasized the human nature of Jesus.

During this period, three noted Anglican scholars, all fellows of Trinity College, Cambridge—Joseph Barber Lightfoot, Brooke Foss Westcott, and Fenton John Anthony Hort—did serious historical studies of the New Testament and the writings of the church fathers. One unfortunate victim of the new critical attitude toward the Bible, however, was John William Colenso, bishop of Natal. After publishing a study that shed doubt on the Book of Genesis, he was charged with heresy by his superior, the bishop of Cape Town. Then followed a series of complicated legal battles, culminating in the deposition of Bishop Colenso by his English counterparts.

At home, this questioning spirit within the church prompted a resurgence of the Anglo-Catholicism initiated by the Oxford Movement. In 1889 a group of young Oxford scholars published a book of essays, Lux Mundi (Light of the World), which sought to demonstrate that the results of modern critical studies of scripture were not inconsistent with the principles of Anglo-Catholicism.

Over the years, the Anglo-Catholics had introduced many modifications and much ceremonial into church ritual. To this there was a great deal of low church resistance. Under the Public Worship Regulation Act of 1874, clergymen could be sent to prison for irregularities in the service, and some Anglo-Catholics were so imprisoned—to great public indignation. Finally, in 1890 the archbishop of Canterbury, sitting in his own court—for the first time in two hundred years—sanc-

tioned those ritualistic changes that had historic precedent and overturned judgments against the bishop of
Lincoln, arising from charges of ritualistic change.

In all, then, the nineteenth century transformed the
Church of England. Although for many it remained the
comfortable, complacent church of the English country
squires, nonetheless by century's end it had been considerably energized and renewed, both in its evangelical spirit and in its ritual character. It had also
become the mother church of a growing international
family of churches. The twentieth century would bring
equally significant changes.

IV

The English Church in the Early Twentieth Century

AS THE TWENTIETH CENTURY BEGAN IN ENGLAND, QUEEN
Victoria's son succeeded her to the throne as King Edward VII, at the age of fifty-nine. He was a genial,
gregarious man, and during his reign there was considerable reaction against straitlaced Victorianism. Indeed, it is customary to think of Edward and the
Edwardians as elegant persons of somewhat loose behavior. But Edward, like his countrymen, had his serious side, and his personal diplomacy did much to
stave off World War I.

War did come—though not before Edward's death in
1910. It was to be the first in a series of social and

31

political upheavals—followed by the Great Depression, and then World War II—that would change the face of England, indeed the world, forever. By midcentury the British Empire had broken apart and England was neither a political nor an economic world power any more.

These monumental events left their mark on the Church of England. One area so affected was the church's attitude to social reform. For a time in the mid-nineteenth century, Frederick Maurice and a group of other broad churchmen had led a Christian Socialist movement. In 1889 the Christian Social Union was formed, to be joined in 1906 by the Anglican Church Socialist League, allied to the Labour party. Remnants of the Christian Social Union were transformed into the Industrial Christian Fellowship in 1919. By the interwar years, the Anglo-Catholic Order of the Church Militant could accept socialism as the natural economic aspect of Christianity. The general social concerns of the church were expressed in the Malvern Declaration, drawn up in 1941 under the direction of Archbishop William Temple. These foreshadowed the implementation of a socialistic national welfare state policy after World War II.

Intellectually, the early twentieth century saw the spread of free-thinking, skeptical ideas toward Biblical matters. In extreme liberal or modernist circles, the miraculous element was all but dismissed from the church, and Christ became simply a good man and a wise teacher. Such views were not acceptable to the church at large, and most liberal churchmen would not publicly endorse them, though many were privately sympathetic. One man did make the attempt. In 1911, J. M. Thompson of Magdalen College, Oxford, pub-

lished *Miracles in the New Testament*, denying the
existence of such phenomena. As a result he was forced
to give up his ministry. Moderately liberal views, however, found more toleration as the century wore on.

The Anglo-Catholic response to a world in crisis was
to increase the emphasis on the spiritual resources of
the church. Thus, Anglo-Catholics stressed historical
tradition, the sacramental nature of the church, and the
importance of ritual. This approach seems to have ap-
pealed to clergy more than to laymen, and opposition
to changes in ritual continued. As early as 1904, a royal
commission on ecclesiastical discipline reported many
abuses by the Anglo-Catholics.

At the same time, the commission observed that the
law on public worship in the church was "too narrow,"
and urged revision of the prayerbook to allow a wider
range of ritualistic practice. In response, the church
Convocations began a twenty-year effort to create a new
prayerbook. When the new book was ready, it aroused
considerable resistance, some claiming that it went too
far toward the Anglo-Catholic position, others that it
did not go far enough. The House of Commons rejected
the book in 1927 and again in 1928.

The bishops, however, resolved unofficially to permit
deviation from the older, approved prayerbook along
the lines of the 1928 version. In practice, there was
considerable toleration, and much of the controversy
faded away. Ultimately, the Anglo-Catholics had succeeded in making Anglican church services considerably more elaborate.

To meet the demands of the time, the church also
needed a new structure which would free it to some
degree from government control and which would al-

low the laity a greater voice in the management of church affairs. In 1919, Parliament passed an Enabling Act, which created a National Assembly of the church to debate on matters relating to the church and pass judgments on to Parliament. This National Assembly consisted of three houses: bishops, clergy (derived from the Convocations), and laity. The lay members were to be chosen by parish councils and Diocesan Conferences, which themselves had a role in managing local church affairs. The Convocations continued to meet separately to deal with matters of worship and doctrine.

Changing circumstances also forced the independent churches of the wider Anglican Communion to organize themselves more formally. One by one, the old missionary provinces of the church had emerged as new, independent churches, which remained in joint communion with the see of Canterbury and recognized the spiritual primacy of the archbishop. As these churches grew in number it became more and more necessary for them to confer. Hence, in 1867 the archbishop of Canterbury held a conference at Lambeth Palace, his London residence, to which all the bishops of the churches of the Anglican Communion were invited. This meeting proved so useful that similar conferences have since been held at roughly ten-year intervals. In the twentieth century, they have played a particularly important role in holding these churches together.

In 1897 a Consultative Body of the Lambeth Conference was formed to handle matters relevant to the conference between meetings, and in 1948 an Advisory Council on Missionary Strategy was established to coordinate the activities of the various churches. Also, in 1959, the first executive secretary for the Anglican Communion, a bishop of the Episcopal Church of the United States, was named to coordinate activities in these two areas of concern. In addition to the Lambeth Conferences, worldwide congresses of the church, attended by clergy and laymen as well as bishops, were held in London in 1908, in Minneapolis in 1954, and in Toronto in 1963.

Because of their special position, balanced between the Roman Catholic and the Protestant churches, and because of their own experience as a group of independent churches joined in common fellowship, the churches of the Anglican Communion had long been interested in ecumenism—the movement toward the reunification of churches. Fittingly, they took an active role in the events that led to the formation of the World Council of Churches, and when that group first met in 1948, the archbishop of Canterbury inaugurated the meeting with a prayer.

The Anglican Communion's official position on union with other churches is contained in the Lambeth Quadrilateral, which was approved by the Lambeth Conference of 1888, and reaffirmed by that of 1920. First established by the American Episcopal church, this formulation calls for belief in holy scripture, the Apostles' and Nicene Creeds, and the sacraments of baptism and Holy Communion, as well as adherence to the historical line of bishops as the basis for any unification of churches.

The Eastern Orthodox churches and the Churches of Sweden and Finland all maintain the historical episcopacy. Relations between them and the churches of the Anglican Communion, therefore, have long been cordial. Full intercommunion of the Anglican churches with the Old Catholic churches of Central Europe was reached in 1931. With the Roman Catholic church lengthy discussions were held at Malines, Belgium, in 1925 and 1926, but without immediate result.

For the major Protestant churches, on the other hand, which gave up the episcopacy during the Reformation, the Lambeth Quadrilateral poses real difficulties to union. Yet the Anglican Communion recognizes the validity of the ministry of the other Protestant churches within those churches, and has held talks on unity with several of them.

One instance of particularly close Anglican association is the Church of South India, a regional church formed in 1947 from the union of Anglican, Methodist, Presbyterian, and Congregational churches. The resulting church is not officially Anglican—the Anglican diocese involved left the Anglican Communion, with its approval, at the time of union—but it does have bishops in the historical line. Although many Anglicans initially felt considerable hesitancy over the status of its clergy, the Church of South India is now in full communion with the Anglican fellowship.

The Church of England was profoundly affected by World War II. Like the nation as a whole, the church faced a formidable task of rebuilding in the aftermath of the war. German bombing had caused massive physical damage. Of seven hundred churches in London, many were destroyed, many more were seriously impaired, and only seventy remained unscathed. Cathedrals, too, were damaged. Of the medieval Coventry Cathedral, only a blackened shell and the spire survived. In addition some 10 percent of Anglican schools were destroyed.

The ranks of the clergy were seriously depleted by the war. Largely because of conscription into the armed forces, ordinations declined sharply—from 562 in 1940 to 158 in the last year of the war.

But even as the church's resources were reduced by the effects of the war, the demands of the postwar world were increasing. England had undertaken a huge housing program—one million new homes were built by 1951 and another million by 1955. These large urban and suburban housing tracts needed church buildings as well, and an active ministry to serve their inhabitants.

To meet these various demands, the church, under Archbishop Geoffrey Fisher, began a major effort of rebuilding. In one typical diocese, in which more than one hundred churches, church halls, and parsonages had been severely damaged, repairs were completed by 1952 at a cost of a quarter of a million pounds. The diocese then built twenty-one new churches, sixteen new halls, and sixteen parsonages within the next ten years, spending another million and three-quarter pounds in the process.

Cathedrals were also restored. A dramatic new cathedral was constructed at Coventry, incorporating the shell of the old building as an open court. New cathedrals also were constructed at Guildford and Liverpool; elsewhere, older cathedrals were enlarged, and parish churches were expanded and converted into cathedrals.

The English church and state cooperated in the postwar reconstruction of the country's schools. The government's postwar Education Act established various categories of schools, involving differing degrees of state and church control and financial support. Large sums were spent restoring and rebuilding the church schools, and some were now turned over completely to state control (and support).

Immediately after the war, the ordination of clergy returned to prewar levels, although it later began to lag and the number of theological colleges was reduced. Special efforts were made to provide a church presence in urban housing tracts, and rural parishes with declining membership were combined to maintain pastoral care.

By midcentury, then, the Church of England had effectively recovered from the war. Its chief problem was now to demonstrate its relevance in the postwar world.

V

The Modern English Church

BRITAIN IN THE SECOND HALF OF THE TWENTIETH CEN-
tury was scarcely recognizable as the imperial
heartland which had ended the previous century in
celebration of Queen Victoria's diamond jubilee, drawing visitors from around the world. By 1950, the largest
colonial dependencies had broken away. Yet, the Suez
invasion of 1956 and the Falklands War of 1982 were
brave attempts to show that Britain had not quite abandoned the international stage. In the meantime, the
cold war and the threat of nuclear annihilation over-
shadowed the world.

New domestic tensions became apparent. Liberal im-
migration policies brought many people from the former colonies to Britain in the middle decades of the
century. During the economic recession which beset

the developed world in the 1970s, they became targets of the racist violence which provided an easy outlet for deep-seated bitterness and insecurity among the local population. Moreover, marked social changes, both legal and attitudinal, brought to the fore subjects which had previously been taboo, such as divorce, abortion, and homosexuality.

Faced with this bewildering array of external situations and with a steady decline in its own membership, the Church of England, as a national church, was expected to produce meaningful suggestions, if not solutions.

To adapt to the new conditions, the Church of England first considered internal affairs. It began by revising the canon law of the church, the statutes that had governed its administration for some three hundred years in virtually unchanged form. In a major effort extending over twenty years, the canons were thoroughly rewritten with the aim of making the legal procedures—including the ecclesiastical courts—more applicable to modern issues.

Having reorganized its judicial system, the church turned to its legislative structure. By the 1950s it had become clear that the church assembly system, introduced in 1919, was too cumbersome and too distant from parish concerns to provide effective government. After much discussion, a new synodical system was introduced in 1969. It called for a smaller, more streamlined, three-house General Synod—of bishops, clergy, and laity (retaining nominally the division of bishops and clergy into the Convocations of York and Canterbury). It also introduced synodical government at the local and the diocesan levels.

The executive branch of the church was also brought up to date. The political appointment of bishops had long been a troubling matter for Anglicans, but it seemed inevitable for an established church. As supreme governor of the church, the queen made the appointments, and she could act only on the advice of "her" government, i.e. the prime minister. But it was agreed in 1976 that final selection of a bishop would be made from two names submitted by a Crown appointments commission, consisting of the archbishops, elected delegates from the General Synod, and members selected by the local diocese.

In sum, these measures gave the church considerable control over its own affairs, while maintaining its status as an established church. But in some ways, they also emphasized the dual nature of the church: as a national church, serving the country as a whole; and as a denominational church, dedicated to the spiritual needs of its own active members. While the new synodical government brought the laity more strongly into church administration, the laity so involved were inevitably those already most active in the church's affairs. A shrinking minority, they stood in sharp contrast to the population at large, many of whom instinctively identified themselves as Anglicans, or "C of E," but attended church only for baptisms, weddings, and funerals.

The latter part of the twentieth century brought new considerations in church doctrine and changes in church services. During the 1960s Anglicans were caught up in the worldwide Christian debate on the nature of God. (The "death of God" was the cry of the most liberal group.) The public focus of the controversy was the book *Honest to God* by John Robinson, bishop of Woolwich. Among other things, the bishop called for his readers to rethink God as residing within themselves rather than being "out there."

In the 1970s the focus of the debate shifted to the nature of Christ, and academic theologians were preoccupied with "Christology." Again extreme positions were announced. Some Anglicans insisted that Jesus was a fully human being, by whom the divine presence was made manifest. Public attention was caught by a volume entitled *The Myth of God Incarnate*, in which a number of prominent Anglican theologians announced their acceptance of the new views concerning the nature of Christ. No settled opinion was ever reached, and the debate revealed once more that within Anglicanism a variety of opinions could be tolerated.

In the 1960s there was great interest in the revision of the liturgy that regulated the services of the church. Like that of many other Christian churches, Anglican scholarship had, over the years, revealed much that had been unknown or forgotten about the early rituals of the church. And Anglicans, like others, were concerned to present liturgical language in a form that could communicate more directly with modern churchgoers.

One of the first expressions of this effort grew out of a new understanding of the central place of Holy Communion, now more commonly called the Eucharist, in the rites of the early church. Liturgical emphasis in the communion service was shifted from sacrifice to celebration. In many parishes the new communion service became the regular form of Sunday worship rather than the traditional morning prayer.

The most significant changes of all, however, were in

the venerable prayerbook. In use since 1662—and re-
vered by Anglicans even more than the King James
Bible—the *Book of Common Prayer* increasingly became the focus of those who wanted to change both the
character of church ritual and the language in which it
was presented. Mindful of the problems with Parliament in 1928, the reformers moved with caution. In the
1960s alternate "Series 2" services were developed for
"experimental" use, and by the 1970s "Series 3" services had been prepared, departing even further from
the 1662 prayerbook. Ultimately these were incorporated in the *Alternative Service Book*, formally introduced in 1980. Although the old prayerbook was officially retained, there was no doubt the church au-
thorities expected parishes to use the new formulation,
and most of them did so.

The changes provoked an outcry among the laity and
in Parliament. Many demanded the retention of
Thomas Cranmer's prayerbook and also of the King
James' Bible, which was now being replaced by con-
temporary-language versions. Some 600 individuals,
representing diverse aspects of the nation's cultural life,
signed a petition against the modernized texts. And in
1981 Parliament seriously debated a Prayerbook Protec-
tion Bill that would have forced every parish to employ
the old *Book of Common Prayer* at least once a month
for its main service.

Like the administrative reorganizations from which
it stemmed, the conflict emphasized the split role of the
church, as repository of national traditions and as living church. Those who rarely attended church service
were bewildered by the cumulative changes and saw
only abrogation of their venerable national heritage.

Those active in the day-to-day life of the church, however, saw efforts to improve its ministry to a changing world.

For Anglican traditionalists, the 1970s and 1980s held even greater shocks. The worldwide Charismatic movement found growing numbers of adherents among Anglicans. Also called *Pentecostal*, after the experience of the Apostles, who received the Holy Spirit on Pentecost, fifty days after Easter, this movement had begun among the more fundamentalist Protestant churches in the early decades of the century. By the 1960s, it had spread to such "mainline" churches as the Baptist, the Methodist, and the Roman Catholic. In the Church of England, the movement surfaced early in the decade and by the late 1970s it was said to have more than 800,000 adherents. The central Charismatic experience is a *spirit baptism*, an experience of conversion (with a sense of being *born again*). One of the chief marks of the experience, or Charismatic *gifts*, is *speaking in tongues*, a babbling quasi-speech that seems to issue involuntarily (and is believed by some to represent some ancient language). Others are *healing* (faith healing) and *prophesying*, which is not foretelling the future, but spontaneous utterance that purports to be directly inspired by the Holy Spirit.

On occasion, charismatic groups have marked themselves off from others in the church, and the movement has been divisive in some parishes. Nevertheless, on the whole, charismatic renewal has energized the Church of England and has in recent years provided a dynamism many found sorely lacking.

In some quarters, charismatic concern in the 1970s

shifted to demonic possession. Popular novels and films at the time fueled interest in the practice of demonic exorcism. Some clergy were drawn into rites of exorcism, and several of these ended tragically. In 1975 the archbishop of Canterbury issued guidelines severely limiting such practices.

Most political issues of the latter half of the twentieth century found the church, like the nation, divided. While Anglicans generally were supportive of the government's position on the cold war, a great many were active in the Campaign for Nuclear Disarmament in the 1950s and 1960s. Churchmen spoke both for and against the government in the Suez invasion of 1956. In 1982 the church provoked considerable animosity by converting the government's jingoistic plans for a Falklands victory service into a more restrained service of thanksgiving. The on-going troubles of Northern Ireland were especially close to home and the continuation of apartheid in South Africa was also troublesome.

Churchmen also became involved in a variety of social issues, from the dangers of water and air pollution to the corruption of the young by popular music. Appropriately, much of the church's official concern was for the socially disadvantaged, both urban and rural. Special ministries were established in economically troubled areas, and local industrial missions extended the reach of the church still further. The Social and Industrial Commission, organized by the church in 1923, was reconstituted in 1951 as the Social and Industrial Council, dedicated to exploring the role of the church in the fields of labor and industry.

The proliferation of racial minorities in postwar Britain posed novel problems as increasing numbers of dark-skinned immigrants entered the country. The first race riots were seen in the late 1950s, and national efforts to ameliorate the situation were joined by Anglicans. In 1947 the General Synod had called for the recognition of Britain as a multiracial society and urged the government to engage in "policies of positive discrimination" towards minority groups. In 1980 a resource group was created specifically to aid churchpeople in furthering the goal of a harmonious, multiracial society.

As a bastion of traditional family values, the church has been resistant to the complex issues posed by the women's movement. Even in the 1980s, its position on divorce—especially remarriage of divorced persons—remained little changed from the time when the church was instrumental in securing the abdication of Edward VIII to "marry the woman [he] loved." Similar church influence was believed to have had a part in the decision of Princess Margaret in 1955 not to marry the divorced Group Captain Peter Townsend. Although divorces have become ever more common in England, the General Synod has continued to oppose remarriage in the church.

Abortions became increasingly common in Britain after the Abortion Act of 1967. This act legalized abortion on a number of grounds, including consideration of the woman's "total environment, actual or reasonably foreseeable." But the church continued to express its disapproval and in the 1970s, supported legislation to tighten restrictions on abortions.

To calls for an increased role for women in the ministry, the church made some small concessions. It ac-
corded women lay readers equal status with men and
improved salaries, working conditions, and pensions
for women churchworkers. Finally, it approved women
as deacons. But it repeatedly drew the line at the ordination of women to the full priesthood.

Alternate lifestyles, including unmarried mixed couples and gays living together, aroused guarded sympathy from the church, but no real acceptance. Some
individual churchmen were involved in groups supporting gay rights, and the church never denounced
homosexuality as such. But it did assert that such activity "fell short of the Christian ideal," and it failed to
endorse homosexual unions as an acceptable alternative to heterosexual ones.

Whatever its stand on social issues, the church did
endeavor to reach as many people as possible with its
evangelical activities. The postwar years began with
frank recognition that religion had become, for the great
majority of English people, "simply irrelevant to the
question of living." Accordingly, in 1945 a church commission issued an ambitious program entitled *Towards
the Conversion of England.* Some thirty years later, after
intensive efforts to implement these ideas, a religious
census found the Church of England slowly but steadily losing numbers.

It was clearly not for want of trying that the Church
of England was unable even to hold its own. As we have
seen, efforts were made to reach disaffected groups,
and special ministries were instituted for such purposes. The church also sought to utilize the media,

working first with BBC radio, then with BBC television, to bring its message to the nation. Indeed, the evangelical effort was recognized as an essential element of the church's mission. The lesson that church evangelicals had sought to teach for more than a century had apparently been absorbed by the church at large.

Even the changes that had been instituted in the prayerbook and ritual practice had been designed to emphasize the living significance of the church. The reintroduction of the Eucharist as the chief form of worship, and the family-centered character of that worship, aimed to make the Christian family in the local parish both the heart of the church and its hope for the future—its center for outreach into the local community.

The Church of England had, of necessity, to direct its attention outward, as well as focus on its own doctrinal concerns and events within the country. One immediate concern in the postwar years was the larger Anglican Communion. In 1949, after a gap of nearly twenty years, the Lambeth Conferences were resumed, setting in motion processes which would lead to the worldwide Anglican Communion of churches we know today. (That body of independent but allied churches we will examine more closely in Part Three of this book.) Indeed, the archbishop of Canterbury increasingly found himself cast as the spiritual head and unifying symbolic center for the wider communion.

Ecumenical relations were also an important part of the Church of England's activities in these years. In 1946 Archbishop Fisher preached a sermon calling for certain other churches to "take Episcopacy into their system" as a way of achieving unity. The Methodists responded favorably, and a twenty-year dialogue was begun with the aim of unifying the two churches. Despite approval by the Methodists, the effort foundered on close votes in the Anglican Synod in 1972. A decade later a scheme for unity with the United Reformed church met a like fate.

One often-cited reason for reluctance on the part of some Anglicans to unite with other Protestant churches was a fear of disturbing the growing relationship with the Roman Catholic church. An unofficial visit by Archbishop Geoffrey Fisher to the Vatican in 1961, and an official one by Archbishop Michael Ramsey in 1966, led to the establishment of an Anglican-Roman Catholic International Commission to explore areas of agreement between the two churches. In time the commission reached joint statements on the Eucharist and the ministry, and on authority within the church.

Discussion with the Orthodox churches also continued, with the establishment of an Anglican-Orthodox Doctrinal Commission in 1962. Here the Anglicans agreed to accept the Orthodox position by deleting the phrase "and the Son" from the Nicene Creed at some future date, on the grounds that it had not originally been present. (Any movement toward fuller alignment with the Orthodox churches, however, has been delayed by the ordination of women priests in some churches of the Anglican Communion.)

In addition to its dialogues with other churches, Anglicans have also engaged in wider ecumenical movements. The Church of England still maintains a strong presence in the British Council of Churches and the World Council of Churches. In addition, many of the changes in the Church of England, liturgical and otherwise, have their counterpart in other Christian churches. Incorporation of new biblical scholarship and new understanding of the ritual practices of the early church, together with moves to incorporate language closer to the everyday language of churchgoers, all tend to make services more alike. (The Roman Catholic adoption of local vernaculars instead of Latin is but one example.)

Anglicans anticipate that, regardless of the outcome of specific movements toward unity between individual churches, the churches of Christendom in their reactions to common problems in the modern world are simply becoming more alike. As Archbishop Geoffrey Fisher is reported to have said to Pope John XXIII during his visit in 1961, "We are each now running on parallel courses; we are looking forward until, in God's good time, our two courses approximate and meet."

PART TWO

THE EPISCOPAL CHURCH IN THE UNITED STATES

VI

In America, a New Beginning

THE BRITISH SEA CAPTAINS, EXPLORERS, AND ADVEN-
turers who sailed to America in the sixteenth century
brought their prayers and sometimes their ministers
with them. Surprisingly, the first place within the present United States at which the Anglican Holy Communion was celebrated was San Francisco. This was in
1579, while Sir Francis Drake was anchored in his ship
the *Pelican* (later named the *Golden Hind*), on his voy-
age around the world.

The earliest successful British settlements were
Jamestown, Virginia, in 1607, and the Plymouth
Colony in Massachusetts in 1620. The history of the
English church in America properly begins with these
events. Both groups of settlers were Puritans. The An-

glicans at Jamestown, however, followed the prayer-book and remained with their native church, while the settlers in Massachusetts were Separatists. These were the pilgrim fathers, who had fled England first for the Netherlands, then for the New World, seeking a place where they could worship as they chose. This fundamental difference was to mark much of the history of the colonial church in America.

The legendary Captain John Smith, one of the founders of Jamestown, brought with him his chaplain, the Reverend Robert Hunt. Chaplain Hunt presided over the building of a church, conducted regular services, and acted as a peacemaker among the quarreling colonists. He survived less than a year. In fact, the troubled colony nearly perished as a whole, but was saved in 1610 by the timely arrival of Lord Delaware, with more colonists. A new chaplain was installed, the church was repaired, and religious life resumed.

In 1611 a second parish was established in Virginia. It was the minister of this parish who baptized Pocahontas, the Indian maiden known to us today for having saved the life of Captain John Smith when he was captured by her father, the great chief Powhatan. Several years later, four more ministers were sent to the new colony.

In 1624, King James revoked the charter of the Virginia Company and converted the settlement into a royal colony. This event established the Church of England in Virginia. In practice, this meant little alteration in the life of the fledgling church. Most early Virginia clergymen, both before and after the establishment, adhered to the prayerbook but sympathized with the Calvinists. Now, however, direction of the church passed from the Virginia Company to the colony's legislature, the House of Burgesses. Control of local parishes fell to elected vestries, which appointed ministers and often retained authority over them by limiting tenure to one year at a time.

The Great Rebellion and the declaration of the Commonwealth in England made little difference to the church in Virginia. The prayerbook was still used— with the omission of prayers for the king—and the House of Burgesses retained its authority. In fact, the Anglicans' presence in the colony was considerably increased by loyalists who fled to Virginia to escape the Commonwealth.

Following the Restoration, the old relationship with the English church was resumed. By custom, general responsibility for the colonial church had fallen to the bishop of London. Feeling the lack of bishops to regulate the church in the New World, he now decided to appoint commissaries to represent him. The first of these, James Blair, was appointed commissary for Virginia in 1689. He did much for the new church, and by 1707 had increased the number of ministers from twenty-two to forty. He also founded the College of William and Mary at Williamsburg, having convinced the House of Burgesses that they should have a school to train their own ministers, instead of depending solely on England.

The next colony to espouse Anglicanism was Maryland. Lord Baltimore had established the colony in 1634 as a haven for English Roman Catholics. The first Anglican clergyman only arrived in 1650, and there were still few clergy in 1696 when Thomas Bray was appointed commissary. Although Bray was unable to journey to the colony himself until 1700, he had nevertheless increased the number of clergy there to sixteen by that time. Largely through his efforts, the church was established in Maryland in 1702. By the time of the Revolution, Virginia and Maryland together had half of the 250 Anglican clergy in America.

Thomas Bray performed his greatest service to America in England, with the founding of the Society for Promoting Christian Knowledge (SPCK), and the Society for the Propagation of the Gospel (SPG). He had recognized the need for the SPCK when he discovered that the clergy he recruited for Maryland were too poor to provide their own libraries. Once in America, he soon saw a role for the SPG in bringing missionaries to English settlers outside the regular parishes, and also to serve the Indians and the Negro slaves. From the time of its founding, the SPG played a major part in the development of the church in the colonies.

Outside of Virginia and Maryland, Anglican activity in the South focused on Charlestown, South Carolina, which had its first English church in 1681. In 1709 Anglicanism was officially established in the colony.

Both Georgia and North Carolina were settled later, and the church took root slowly in these colonies, largely through the efforts of missionaries of the SPG. Though the church was legally established in North Carolina in 1765, it was not yet a significant factor in the life of the colony at the time of the Revolution.

The church fared somewhat better in Georgia, where there was an Anglican minister in Savannah from the founding of the colony in 1732. Among the early incumbents of this office were John Wesley and George

Whitefield, both later to be involved in the development of Methodism. Yet, by 1776, the only strong parishes were in Savannah and Augusta.

The situation was very different in the north. As
Virginia was the colonial heart of the Anglican church,
so Massachusetts was the homeland of the Dissenters.
The original pilgrim fathers who settled at Plymouth
were soon joined by one thousand more dissenting
Puritans, settling in Boston and some half dozen other
villages in the Massachusetts Bay area. In 1691 the
Plymouth Colony was absorbed into the larger Massachusetts Bay Colony.

It is tempting to consider the Puritan settlers as
champions of religious freedom, but nothing could be
further from the truth. The Puritans, who had sacrificed
so much to escape from the Church of England, were
determined to exclude all trace of it from within their
borders. They drove out the churchmen they found
already living in the Boston area, and for years forbade
any others from settling. Even Nonconformists, such as
Roger Williams, who held his own Puritan views, were
forced to leave.

Still, the Puritan colony in Massachusetts flourished,
economically and intellectually. By 1700 it was by far
the most populous colony. The Congregationalists, as
the Puritans came to be called, dominated the intellectual life of New England. A single family produced
three successive generations of formidable ministers,
Richard, Increase, and Cotton Mather. Harvard College
was founded at Cambridge in 1636, and in 1640 the
Bay Psalm Book was published, the first book to be
printed in the colonies.

The English churchmen could hardly ignore so great

a prize. When James II sent a new president to the colony of Massachusetts in 1685, the president was accompanied by the Reverend Robert Tacliffe, who conducted Anglican services in a townhouse in Boston. Within a month he had organized a congregation, and four years later, the first Anglican church opened in Boston. The newly formed SPG quickly turned its attention to New England, dispatching a number of missionaries to Massachusetts. By the time of the Revolution, there were three parishes in Boston alone, and a dozen throughout Massachusetts.

Ironically, in Massachusetts—and in Connecticut—the Congregational churches were established by law, and it was the Anglicans who often found themselves taxed to support an established church other than their own. Another source of tension between the two groups was the fact that many of the northern Anglican ministers were high churchmen, at the furthest extreme from their Puritan neighbors. Also, the Anglican missionaries of the SPG were much resented by the Congregationalists, who thought it improper to send missionaries among people who were already Christian. Still, the Anglicans made considerable headway, even in the heartlands of the dissenting colonies.

If the Anglican church in the north was least welcome in Massachusetts, it was most tolerated in New York. After the British took the colony from the Dutch in 1664, both Dutch and British services were held in the church of the fort that dominated Manhattan island. In 1694 the Colonial Assembly voted to support Protestant ministers by taxes in four New York counties. Although much of the population consisted of Dissenters, the first minister appointed for New York City under the new act was an Anglican, William Vesey, who had been educated at Harvard College. The SPG was particularly active in the colony, and by 1776 it had supported fifty-eight ministers there. In 1754, an Anglican academy, King's College—later to become Columbia University—was built "on the skirts of the city."

Pennsylvania was founded by and for the Quakers, but religious freedom was given to all. One of the first Anglican missionaries sent by the SPG was George Keith, a former Quaker who had converted to Anglicanism. Through his influence, many more Quakers entered the church. The first Anglican church building in Philadelphia was erected in 1695, and by 1700 the parish had five hundred members. The College and Academy, which would become the University of Pennsylvania, was founded in 1749. It was not a church institution, but it had an Anglican minister as provost.

Connecticut was initially unreceptive to Anglicans. The Congregational church was established by law, and persons who attended services led by Anglican missionaries were liable to fines. Under these severe circumstances, an astonishing event occurred at the graduation ceremonies of the Congregational Yale University in 1722. The president of the university, Timothy Cutler, announced that he and three other Congregational ministers had grave doubts about the validity of the Congregational ministry and would leave for England to seek Anglican ordination. When Cutler returned from England, he became rector at Christ Church in Boston, where he remained for more than forty years. In Connecticut, this marked a turning point from which the Anglican church grew steadily. There were seven ministers in the colony in 1742, twenty by 1776.

During most of the colonial period, both Maine and New Hampshire were under the domination of Massachusetts, which effectively kept out most Anglican clergy. Yet, isolated missionaries considerably extended the reach of the church in both colonies, especially after New Hampshire was freed from Massachusetts' control, in 1741.

Rhode Island, the colony founded by Roger Williams when he was driven from Massachusetts, was open to all except Roman Catholics and Quakers. The first Anglican services were held in 1698, and with the help of the SPG, the church did well there.

Similarly, the SPG was active in Delaware and New Jersey. The churches there were closely linked to those in Pennsylvania, and missionaries moved back and forth freely among the parishes.

Although the Anglican church grew and spread in the American colonies, it had powerful rivals, which outnumbered it in many localities. There was the Congregational church in Massachusetts and Connecticut, and the Roman Catholic church, which was favored in Maryland. In Pennsylvania, there were Quakers and a number of German Protestant churches. There were Scotch-Irish Presbyterians in the middle colonies, Huguenots in South Carolina and New York, Dutch Reformed churchmen in New York and New Jersey, and Baptists in many colonies, especially in the South.

A challenge of a new kind faced all the Protestant churches in the colonies, including the Anglicans, in the 1730s and 1740s, in the form of a powerful religious revival, known as the Great Awakening. This outburst of impassioned preaching and wholesale conversion was inspired by the preaching of the Congregationalist, Jonathan Edwards, but soon spread to the Baptists and to the Presbyterians, among whom converts were known as *new lights*. Within the Anglican church, the Great Awakening was led by George Whitefield, a follower of John Wesley, who had orchestrated a similar movement in England. Whitefield traveled throughout the colonies, preaching to large crowds in Anglican churches, halls, and the open air. The Great Awakening was a mixed blessing for the Anglican church in America. At first it led to many new converts and widened the base of the church. But many of the converts were not content with the staid Anglican style, and ultimately the followers of Wesley and Whitefield withdrew to form the new Methodist Episcopal church in 1784.

Throughout the troubles of the colonial period, the Anglican church was severely hampered by the lack of bishops in America. For an *episcopal* church to be without bishops was indeed a contradiction in terms, yet such was the state of the colonial church for 175 years. It caused enormous practical difficulties, chief among which was the problem of obtaining clergy, who had to be consecrated by a bishop. For Americans wishing to become clergymen, this meant a long, tedious, dangerous, and expensive trip to England. For parishes, it often meant finding an Englishman who was willing to emigrate, and sometimes these were not the best qualified. Instead, many parishes depended on lay readers or missionaries from the SPG and consequently had to forego the pastoral benefits of having their own parish priest.

Then, there was the matter of church discipline and spiritual leadership, both of which were normally supplied by the bishop. The clergy in America were often alone, isolated from such guidance.

The situation prompted American clergy to appeal to England from time to time for their own bishops. On several occasions, the need was recognized and seemed about to be met, but the expected action was always aborted. In 1638 Archbishop Laud had planned to create a bishop of New England, but the Great Rebellion intervened and the archbishop lost his head. A bishop of Virginia was to be named in 1673, but the British cabinet fell, and the new ministry did not pursue the initiative. Over the next century, a half dozen other attempts to create bishops for America likewise came to nothing.

Part of the reason for the failures was political. To the Dissenters in the New World, the bishops were the most potent symbol of all they had come to hate and fear in the English church. Each call for American bishops brought forth vituperative attacks from the American Congregationalists and their Dissenter allies in England, who were not without political influence.

For Americans loyal to the crown, the appointment of American bishops meant a welcome strengthening of British control over the colonies. But this political aim came increasingly conflicted with the broader American sympathy toward independence. So American patriots, too, opposed the naming of English bishops for America.

Even in Virginia, the heart of established An-

glicanism in America, there was much lay opposition
to the naming of bishops. This came mainly from the
lay vestries, who had gained control over the colonial
church, and resented the idea of subjection to a higher
local authority. In truth, the northern laymen also had
more influence over church affairs than was customary
in England, and few of them endorsed the call for
bishops either.

There were also real practical problems to the ap-
pointing of American bishops. How were they to be
supported, for instance, in areas where the church was
not established? To assurances that tax revenues would
not be used for the purpose, the Dissenters of the north
were openly skeptical.

When the Revolution began, everything changed.
Daily life was disrupted by the war with England, and
the colonists were torn by conflicting ties. Many of the
Anglican clergy felt the pull of the allegiance they had
sworn to the Crown, and they and many of their parishioners were among the Loyalists, who opposed the Revolution. Naturally, this reflected badly on the church,
especially in the northern colonies.

But as many, if not more, clergy and churchgoers
were on the side of independence. Two-thirds of the
signers of the Declaration of Independence were Anglican. And in Virginia, the vast majority of the clergy
actively supported the Revolution.

The war brought terrible destruction to the Anglican
church, as it did to the country at large. As it neared its
end, many of the Loyalists, both clergy and laymen,
fled the country. Some returned to England. Large numbers settled in Nova Scotia. In Maryland alone, half the

forty English clergymen left. Much church property was badly damaged; some churches were completely destroyed.

Yet, there was hope among the Anglicans who remained that a new, independent church—allied with the English church, but separate from it—could be born in the new country. If this was to be achieved, however, a new church structure would have to be created. The question of bishops and their role in the American church would finally have to be answered.

As it happened, two different schemes for structuring the new church emerged. One began in Connecticut, one of the few states in which a substantial core of clergy survived the war. In 1783 ten of the fourteen clergy met, without any laymen present, to consider their situation. Largely high churchmen, they saw the need for a bishop as their most pressing problem and elected one of their number, Samuel Seabury, to fill that role. He embarked at once for England, but failing to secure consecration from bishops there, he then journeyed to Scotland. On 14 November 1784, he was consecrated by three of the aging Scottish Nonjurors. On his return to Connecticut, Bishop Seabury set about organizing his diocese on the English model.

In the meantime, in other states, the American church was organizing itself along somewhat different lines. The chief architect of this effort was William White, rector of a prominent Philadelphia parish. In 1782, before the end of the war, White had written a pamphlet on church organization, *The Case of the Protestant Episcopal Church in the United States Considered*. White argued that the separate Episcopal parishes should organize—as the nation was being organized—at the state and national levels, with elected representatives of both clergy and laymen to serve at both levels. Fearing that bishops could not be obtained from England, he proposed an elected "superior order," to serve until bishops could be secured.

Following meetings in the various states to lay claim to church property and bring the local parishes together, the first meeting of clerical and lay deputies, along the lines White had suggested, took place in New York City in 1784. The delegates agreed on the continued use of the English prayerbook (suitably modified), recommended that each state should have a bishop, and proposed that the national church should be governed by General Conventions, at which the bishops would sit with clergy and lay delegates.

The first General Convention was held in 1785 in Philadelphia. Bishop Seabury was not asked to preside. As a result, no delegates from Connecticut or the other New England states attended. The convention set up a committee to draft a constitution for the church and revise the liturgy. It requested that the various states proceed to choose bishops and proposed that triennial General Conventions be held, with the first set for 1786. This convention met in two sessions, in Philadelphia in June and again in Wilmington, Delaware, in October. It declared that a constitutional convention of the church would be held in Philadelphia on 28 July 1789.

In England, meanwhile, the church and the government had been wrestling with the problem of consecrating bishops who, not being Englishmen, would neither swear allegiance to the king nor obedience to the archbishop. Finally, they agreed to consecrate three such bishops, enough to initiate the episcopal line in America. (The Scottish bishops who had consecrated Bishop Seabury were considered schismatic by the English, so his case could not set a precedent here.) Following their election by the state conventions, William White and Samuel Provoost of New York were consecrated in England on 4 February 1787. A year later, James Madison of Virginia (not to be confused with the fourth president of the United States) was also consecrated in England.

It appeared at this time that America might have *two* Anglican churches—one in New England, headed by Bishop Seabury, and one in the central and southern states, led by the three new bishops. The two groups did indeed have different views on church government. To Bishop White and his colleagues, Bishop Seabury was unacceptably autocratic, representing what was worst in the English church. But to Bishop Seabury and the Connecticut clergy, the participation of laymen in church government and the diminished role of the bishop undermined the essential Episcopal character of the church. Yet, both sides wished to see a single church in the country, and there was a strong urge toward unification.

The opening session of the Philadelphia constitutional convention at which Bishop White presided met without Bishop Seabury or New England delegates. But one of its first actions was to accept the validity of Bishop Seabury's consecration. He then joined the convention, along with other delegates from Connecticut, Massachusetts, and New Hampshire.

Among its resolutions, the convention adopted a prayerbook based on the English prayerbook of 1662, but with the Consecration Prayer from the Scottish prayerbook. It approved a constitution that called for triennial General Conventions consisting of two houses—a House of Deputies, to include both laymen and clergy from each state; and a House of Bishops, with a bishop elected by each state. The convention also adopted a set of canons regulating the training and conduct of the clergy. The formation of the Protestant Episcopal Church of the United States of America was now complete.

The decisions made by the constitutional convention represented a true compromise. The use of language from the Scottish prayerbook, and certainly the inclusion of a separate House of Bishops would not have come about without the participation of Bishop Seabury. Yet, the chief architect of the new church was surely Bishop White. The active role of lay deputies in church government and the election of bishops were his ideas. Together, Bishops Seabury and White established the Episcopal church as a distinctive American version of the Anglican church.

Fittingly, in 1792 all four bishops of the new church joined in the consecration of Thomas John Claggett of Maryland as the fifth American bishop. From this time on the American line of bishops was self-perpetuating, but continuous with that of the Church of England.

VII

Spanning the Continent

THE EPISCOPAL CHURCH CAME INTO BEING AT ALMOST exactly the same time as the United States. The constitutional convention that established the church took place the year that George Washington took office as first president of the nation. Like the new nation, the Episcopal church was initially weak and uncertain, but over the next two hundred years it would spread across the continent, and its influence would extend around the world.

The Revolution had taken a great toll of the church, in terms of destroyed or abandoned property and a depleted clergy. In many minds the church was still associated with England, and hated for that reason. Typically, church members were urban and well-to-do, sore points in a nation composed largely of poor farmers. By now the Methodists had severed their ties with the Episcopalians. Methodist preachers traveling on the frontier made large numbers of converts while the Episcopalians were still seeking to organize themselves.

The Episcopal church got off to a very slow start. At the time of its founding, only one American in four hundred was an Anglican. At the General Convention of 1800, representatives from only seven dioceses were present, and the two-man House of Bishops met in the bedroom of the local rectory.

Yet, the church had inherent strengths. Though its members were few, many were prominent. Presidents Washington, Jefferson, and Madison were all Episcopalians, as were Chief Justices Jay and Marshall. Moreover, the new democratic structure proved sound and suited to the times. Above all, as we shall see, the presence of bishops—so long a source of contention, was one of the greatest assets to the church.

It was not until after the War of 1812 that the church really began to grow. It is possible that the active participation of American Episcopalians in this second war with England laid to rest any suspicions of Episcopalian disloyalty. Whatever the reason, three new bishops, consecrated between 1811 and 1814, led the church in a remarkable resurgence.

Of these three, Alexander Viets Griswold in 1811 was named bishop of the Eastern Diocese. This included the states of Rhode Island, New Hampshire, Vermont, Massachusetts, and Maine, none of which had enough Episcopalians to warrant establishment of its own di-

ocese. Under Bishop Griswold's leadership, seven of
the thirteen churches in Massachusetts were rebuilt,
and twenty-five new ones were constructed. In Rhode
Island, he increased the number of churches from four
to eighteen; in New Hampshire, from five to nine; in
Maine, from two to five. In Vermont, where there were
no churches at all, his activities led to the building of
twelve. In fact, by 1832, Vermont had become a separate
diocese with its own bishop. After Bishop Griswold's
death in 1843, the other states of his diocese also
gained independent status.

Equally successful was Richard Channing Moore,
consecrated bishop of Virginia in 1814. Although Virginia had been the leading center of Anglican activity
before the Revolution, Bishop Moore found that the
church there had been decimated by the war. Of the
fourteen active parishes left in the state, only half had
rectors of their own. By the time of Bishop Moore's
death, nearly thirty years later, the state was once again
strongly Episcopalian. More than one hundred clergy
served some 170 parishes. The state also had its own
theological seminary, which the bishop had founded in
1824.

In New York State in 1811, John Henry Hobart was
elected assistant to Bishop Benjamin Moore, ninth
bishop in the American line. Following the bishop's
death in 1816, Hobart succeeded him as bishop of New
York and as rector of Trinity Church in New York City,
one of the most important parishes in the nation.
Bishop Hobart traveled far more than his colleagues,
repeatedly visiting even the western outposts of his
diocese. He encouraged missionary work among the
Indians, and increased the number of missionaries

from two to fifty. The number of clergy in New York also grew under his supervision—from twenty-six to 133. More than anyone else, he was responsible for founding the church's first national seminary, the General Theological Seminary. It was established in New York City in 1827, on land given by a professor at the seminary, Clement C. Moore. The son of Bishop Benjamin Moore, he was the author of " 'Twas the Night Before Christmas." Bishop Hobart also founded the Episcopal college in Geneva, New York, that now bears his name. It is the oldest Episcopal college in the nation.

The success of the church at this time was in part due to a new wave of Evangelical enthusiasm that spread rapidly in all the Protestant churches, much as the Great Awakening had done in the previous century. In the United States, as in England at about the same time, the emphasis now was on impassioned preaching and a call for personal salvation. Day-long camp meetings were a favorite practice of American Evangelicals—so-called traveling evangelists—in all churches. Episcopalian evangelists differed mainly in that they used the Episcopal prayerbook and baptized their converts into the Episcopal church. Bishops Griswold and Richard Moore were themselves thoroughgoing Evangelicals. Bishop Hobart was a staunch high churchman, but so evangelical in his preaching style that he was sometimes accused of being "Methodistical."

The early decades of the nineteenth century, then, were a time of great evangelical strength in the Episcopal church. They were followed by a rise in high church influence, partly in response to the Oxford Movement in the English church, but also because of the work of Bishop Hobart and his high church fol-

lowers. Indeed, the Oxford Movement itself had been
partly shaped by an earlier generation of high church
Episcopalians. Bishop Hobart, in particular, had made
a deep impression on Newman, both in terms of his
preaching style and his extensive use of tracts in his
own diocese. In the America of the 1830s, Keble's
Christian Year and the Oxford *Tracts for the Times*
were widely read and discussed. The English Tractarians' emphasis on the apostolic, sacramental, and
catholic character of the church found a warm response
in many Episcopalian hearts. In the diocese of New
York, under Bishop Hobart's successor, Bishop Benjamin Onderdonk, and in the General Theological
Seminary in New York City, the response was particularly strong. The general influence was widespread.
William Whittingham, a high church professor at the
seminary and a Tractarian sympathizer, became Bishop
of Maryland in 1840.

With the appearance of *Tract 90* in 1841, the cessa-
tion of the *tracts,* and rumors of Newman's imminent
departure from the church, events came to a head in the
United States as well. The General Theological Seminary was investigated by the bishop-trustees who suspected that it was the center of a pro-Roman Catholic
conspiracy. The controversy nearly forced the seminary
to close, but the House of Bishops ultimately cleared it
of charges. "We feel it is our duty to declare," they
warned, "that no person should be ordained who is not
well acquainted with the landmarks which separate us
from the Church of Rome."

The General Convention of 1844 was decisive. After
four days of furious debate on the issues associated
with the Oxford Movement, the House of Deputies refused to speak against the Tractarians and declared that

"the Church is not responsible for the errors of individuals, whether they are members of this church or otherwise."

In a sad aftermath of the Tractarian controversy, two of the more prominent high church bishops, the brothers Benjamin and Henry Onderdonk, were suspended from office for personal misconduct. Though doctrinal matters were not involved, there had been much evangelical opposition to both men. Their loss was felt by the high church party. Unlike the situation in England, however, there were few defections from the Episcopal church to Rome. Over a thirty-year period, only one bishop, Levi Silliman Ives of North Carolina, and some twenty-five clergy became Roman Catholics.

The end of the Tractarian troubles by no means bridged the divide between high church and low church. But the affair did teach the church that each fraction contributed in its own way toward the essential character of the church as a whole. As in England, the evangelicals strengthened the preaching of the church and renewed its sense of mission in spreading the gospel. The Tractarians, in their turn, revived the notion of the apostolic church and almost totally revised the look of the church buildings and the services. Churches began to be built in the Gothic style and the interiors were transformed. The cross reappeared, flowers were used as decoration, choirs sang. Candles, and even incense, were burnt. And the clergy once more wore elaborate vestments.

The church was moving geographically, as well. As Americans went west, the Episcopal church followed the settlers in their trek across the continent.

The most prominent early figure in the westward extension of the church was Philander Chase. Selected bishop of Ohio in 1819 by the five clergymen of the state, he struggled to assist the fledgling diocese, traveling 1200 miles and preaching 180 times in his second year as bishop. He even traveled to England to seek financial assistance for his diocese. There the sturdy, handsome frontier bishop attracted much attention—and $30,000, part of which he used to establish Kenyon College and a theological school in Gambier, Ohio.

Autocratic by nature, Bishop Chase aroused much opposition, and in 1830 he resigned in frustration, both as bishop of Ohio and as president of Kenyon College. After a brief respite on a farm in Michigan, Bishop Chase was called to resume his episcopal duties, this time in the newly formed diocese of Illinois, which had three ministers and thirty-nine communicants. Again he traveled to England to secure funds for his diocese, and again he was successful. By 1845, the new diocese had twenty-five clergy and over five hundred members—one thousand in 1848. In Illinois, too, he founded a college, named Jubilee College, but it failed to survive the Civil War.

Another frontier bishop was James Hervey Otey of Tennessee. Six foot four inches tall and an outdoorsman, he was named bishop of Tennessee in 1833, also serving as provisional bishop of Mississippi and Florida. His diocese started out with eight clergymen and 117 communicants. By 1860 it had twenty-seven clergy and five hundred communicants.

In 1820 the Episcopal church established a Domestic and Foreign Missionary Society to support its missionary work. In 1835 the General Convention decided that the entire membership of the church should constitute the missionary society. The same General Convention established the post of missionary bishop, a bishop supported by the church at large for an area not yet organized into dioceses.

The first missionary bishop, named in 1835, was Jackson Kemper. In twenty-five years Bishop Kemper oversaw the development of six new dioceses in the North and West. His area of responsibility was so vast that Bishop Kemper on occasion referred to himself as "Bishop of All Outdoors." A high churchman himself, he encouraged the formation of Nashotah House, a monastery and seminary in Wisconsin. Among the founders, all strongly influenced by the Oxford Movement, was John Henry Hobart, Jr., son of Bishop Hobart.

In the meantime, a second missionary bishop, Leonidas Polk, was named in 1838 with responsibility for the South and Southwest. Bishop Polk worked tirelessly in Arkansas, Mississippi, Louisiana, and Texas. When Louisiana became a diocese in 1841, he was chosen as its bishop. Largely through his efforts, the University of the South was founded in Sewanee, Tennessee, in 1857. During the Civil War, Bishop Polk served as a Confederate general of some distinction. He was killed at Pine Mountain, Georgia, in 1864.

The westward sweep of the church continued. In 1853 it reached the West Coast, with William I. Kip consecrated as bishop of California. The following year, Thomas F. Scott became missionary bishop for Washington and Oregon. The church was now a truly national body.

VIII

Growth and Challenge

THE CIVIL WAR DID NOT SERIOUSLY DISRUPT THE WORK OF the church, though clergy and laymen alike were drawn in on both sides. Bishop McIlvaine of Ohio went to England at the request of President Lincoln as part of a delegation to forestall the British recognition of the Confederacy. Ironically, Bishop McIlvaine had converted Leonidas Polk to the church, while Polk was a cadet at West Point and McIlvaine was chaplain there.

During the war, the southern dioceses met together in convention and adopted their own constitution, prayerbook, and canons. But at the General Convention of 1862 in New York, their names were still called in the roll for they were not considered to have withdrawn from the church. Deputies from Texas, Arkansas, and

North Carolina were present at the convention of 1865, which was described as "wonderfully harmonious." By the next General Convention all the southern dioceses were back.

The war did cause considerable harm to church property. In South Carolina, for example, many churches were burned—some merely damaged, three entirely destroyed.

A further problem was presented by the freed blacks, many of whom needed material assistance and schooling. Individual southern clergy had worked among the black slaves, but now more concerted efforts were called for. The General Convention of 1865 established the Freedman's Commission, which raised more than $26,000 its first year and opened ten schools for blacks in the South. In time, this organization became the Commission on Home Missions to Colored People. By 1890 it supported sixty-two white and forty-four black clergy, and staffed sixty-five general schools for blacks and twelve industrial ones. Between 1866 and 1880, twenty-seven black clergy were ordained, and in 1887 the Bishop Payne Divinity School—named for a black bishop of the church—was opened, specifically to train blacks for the ministry. This school was later closed, and blacks were admitted to all of the regular seminaries.

Episcopalian missionary work among the Indians had begun early in New York State and had been extensive in Wisconsin and Minnesota in the years before the Civil War. The General Convention of 1871 instructed the Board of Missions to create a Commission on Indian Affairs. In 1873 the one hundredth bishop in the American line, William Hobart Hare, was consecrated bishop of Niobrara to work among the Indians of the Dakotas and Nebraska. Here Bishop Hare labored until his death in 1909. Of some twenty-five thousand Indians in the area, about ten thousand were baptized. Among them was Chief Gall, a leader in the massacre of General Custer and his men at the Little Big Horn.

Overseas, the missionary work of the church also accelerated after the Civil War. The first Episcopalian missionary in Africa was a black layman, James Thompson, who began his work in Liberia in 1834. John Payne, for whom the divinity school was named, was consecrated bishop for the area in 1851. When he retired twenty years later, Bishop Payne left nine churches and twenty-two missionary stations in his diocese.

In the 1830s several American missionaries worked in China, and in 1844 William J. Boone was consecrated missionary bishop for that country. The missionary effort there proceeded slowly but steadily. By 1897 there were a number of bishops of the Anglican Communion in China. In 1915 the Chinese Holy Catholic church, Chung Hua Sheng Kung Hui, was formed.

In 1866 Channing Moore Williams was named the first Episcopalian bishop for Japan. By 1890 there were 865 communicants of what is now known as the Nippon Seikokai, the Holy Catholic church of Japan.

The missionary work of the Episcopal church has long found particular support from the women of the church. In 1868 the former Ladies Domestic Missionary Relief Association became the Women's Auxiliary to the Board of Missions, and its work was greatly expanded. Soon every diocese in the church had its own branch of the Women's Auxiliary. One of the chief ways in which the auxiliaries support the missionary effort is through the United Thank Offering, an annual collection of funds specifically designated for church missions.

The resurgence of church activity following the Civil War brought renewed tension between its high and low wings. This time the controversy began with the low church evangelicals who resented the increasing influence of the high church ritualists. The ritualists emphasized the so-called real presence of Christ's body and blood during the celebration of the Holy Communion and demonstrated this belief by *adoration* of the bread and wine during the service. These practices outraged the Evangelicals. They also objected to the use of the traditional word *regeneration* in the baptismal service because it implied that a moral rebirth automatically occured at that time, a belief they did not share.

The controversy came to a head in the General Convention of 1874, which adopted a canon against certain of the practices of the ritualists. Among these was the adoration of the bread and wine during Communion. The "Ritual Canon," however, was intended to promote tolerance of differing practices. Some of its restrictions were abandoned in 1904, and the ritual practices earlier found objectionable became commonplace in the church. Another result of the controversy was the departure of a leading Evangelical, George D. Cummins, assistant bishop of Kentucky, from the church. In 1873 Bishop Cummins and a number of like-minded clergymen established the Reformed Episcopal church, a sect which, in the 1980s, still had eight churches and some six-thousand members.

In the latter part of the nineteenth century the old Evangelicals were largely supplanted by so-called broad churchmen, men of liberal leanings, who were generally low church in outlook but who favored tolerance toward specific beliefs and hoped to hold those with different points of view within the church. Typical of the broad churchmen was Phillips Brooks. Internationally known and enormously popular as a preacher, he was rector of Trinity Church in Boston for more than twenty years. In 1891, shortly before his death, he was consecrated bishop of Massachusetts.

At the same time, high churchmen, known in this period as Anglo-Catholics, opposed the liberalizing moves of the broad churchmen and sought to keep the church within the body of Catholic—though not Roman Catholic—tradition. One of the most eloquent Anglo-Catholics was James DeKoven, who was considered for the episcopacy on numerous occasions but never chosen, probably because of his outspoken support of the Anglo-Catholic position.

Not all the difficulties that the Episcopal church faced in the nineteenth century were internal. Like the Church of England, it found itself challenged by new scientific and historical studies. Scientifically, the most direct challenge was posed by Darwin's *Origin of Species,* which seemed to contradict the Biblical account of creation. For their part, historians proposed to examine the Bible and early church writings as critically as they would any other historical documents. The 1860 publication of *Essays and Reviews* aroused as great a furor in the United States as it had in England. Ultimately, most of the new historical and scientific ideas were accepted in the church without serious difficulty. They were taken up most quickly by the broad churchmen and somewhat later by Anglo-Catholics.

Some believers of the new learning went too far. The Reverend Algernon Crapsy of Rochester, New York, was convicted of heresy for denying the Virgin Birth and asserting that physically Jesus was only a man. Thus, the church showed itself capable of tolerating much in the way of revisionary doctrine, but it could not ignore direct challenge to the essence of its Christian character.

Another challenge to the church was posed by the vast expanse of the American West. In the years after the Civil War the church faced the enormous task of ministering to the people who were filling in the great tracts of nearly vacant land. The Episcopal church did more to meet this need than its size would have warranted. In the fifty years from 1830 to 1880 the national population quadrupled, but the number of communicants in the church increased thirteenfold, from thirty-one to four hundred thousand.

These years also saw a profound alteration in the nature of the American people, and this had new implications for the church. Impoverished Central and Southern Europeans poured into the country in the nineteenth century, finding work mainly in the mills and factories of the increasingly industrial country. The Episcopal church had long been the church of well-to-do Anglo-Saxons. Could it respond to the hordes of new immigrants?

The rise of socialism compounded the problem but in a way also helped to solve it. If Charles Darwin represented one major threat to the church, Karl Marx represented another. The socialists aimed to supplant the church as the hope of the poor and oppressed. Indeed, they derided the church for assisting in the enslavement of the poor, for being—in Marx's often misquoted words—"the opium of the people."

To a degree, the charge was true. Some churchmen in America opposed any social changes at all and, in particular, spoke against trade unions, the chief attempt of workingmen to better their lot. Others in the church were more responsive to new ideas. In the 1860s and 1870s many became involved in the Christian socialist movement, which had begun in England, under Frederick Maurice. They took up the cause of social action, fighting child labor and sweatshops and favoring slum clearance and prison reform.

An unofficial group, the American Church Congress, was organized in 1874 to provide a forum for new ideas, including calls for social change. One speaker before the church congress that year was Henry George, reformer and author of the bestseller *Progress and Poverty*. Five years later the congress held a panel discussion including Christian socialists.

Social action was one impetus for the founding of monastic and religious orders in the church. In 1857 the first permanent religious order for women, the Community of St. Mary, set up a home for abandoned girls. In 1870 it opened a hospital and a school, and in time its work spread across the country and abroad. The sisterhood of St. Margaret began in Boston in 1873, and other organizations soon followed in other parts of the country. In 1889 the church revived the ancient order of deaconesses, a priestly order. In this way, hundreds of women participated in parish and mission work.

The first order for men in the United States was the Society of St. John the Evangelist. Known familiarly as the Cowley fathers, its members came over from England in 1870. The first wholly American order for men, the Order of the Holy Cross, was founded in 1884 out of the Holy Cross Mission in New York City. Other male orders were formed in the following years.

The last great legacy of the nineteenth century to the Episcopal church was its cathedrals. The drive to build cathedrals started with the Anglo-Catholic wing of the church. To the Anglo-Catholics, a bishop could hardly be a bishop without a cathedral to conduct services in. The first procathedral—a parish church used in place of a cathedral—was the Church of the Atonement in Chicago, which was presented to its bishop in 1861. In 1867 the first cornerstone for an American cathedral was laid in Davenport, Iowa. Work on the Cathedral of St. John the Divine in New York City began in 1892 and is not yet finished. When complete, the cathedral will be the largest Gothic structure in the world. The Cathedral of SS. Peter and Paul in Washington, D.C., was started in 1907 and completed in 1990. This structure, which is known as the National Cathedral, serves as the official seat of the presiding bishop of the church and emphasizes the important role of Episcopalians in the country's life.

IX

A Renewal of Mission

THE TWENTIETH CENTURY WROUGHT FURTHER CHANGE IN the church. By 1900 the territory of the United States was thoroughly covered with dioceses and missionary districts. The following years saw the conversion of one missionary district after another into full dioceses, particularly in the West. Also, larger dioceses were divided into smaller ones—no longer was each state a single diocese. (This process had begun in the East in 1839 when the diocese of Western New York was formed from part of the older diocese of New York.)

To help organize the large numbers of new dioceses and missionary districts, the church was divided in 1907 into eight provinces. An additional province in Central America has since brought the number to nine.

Each province is directed by a Provincial Council and a Provincial Synod of bishops and deputies, which meets between General Conventions.

The expansion of American interests abroad led the church into new missionary ventures. The missionary district of Alaska had been created in 1892. With the end of the Spanish-American War in 1898, the church began activities in Puerto Rico, Cuba, and the Philippines. Soon the church followed lay Americans into the Hawaiian Islands, Panama, and the Virgin Islands. Its missionaries also worked throughout Latin America. The church was especially active in Mexico, where there were five dioceses by 1990, and in Brazil. The Igreja Episcopal do Brasil, the Episcopal Church of Brazil, has become an independent member of the Anglican Communion, as has its counterpart in the Philippines.

The major political and social events of the twentieth century—two world wars, the Great Depression, American involvement in Korea and Vietnam, all had their effects on the church. Although military involvement created some problems, it did not lead to serious divisions within the church. If anything, it emerged from them rather more united.

There was some pacifism among Episcopalians, as well as the country at large, during World War I. In fact, the pacifist bishop of Utah was asked to resign because of his outspoken opposition to the war. World War II, however, found the country, including Episcopalians, virtually united. Some four hundred Episcopalian ministers served as chaplains. As the subsequent war in Korea dragged on with no end in sight, popular support slowly eroded. Episcopalians, like the rest of the country, were unhappy at the protracted conflict, and General Eisenhower was elected president in 1952 in part because of his promise to end the war.

The Great Depression, too—although Episcopalians were no less affected than other Americans—left the church with a renewed sense of mission. We have seen the beginnings of the Christian socialist movement within the church in the nineteenth century. Such activities continued in the early twentieth century. The Church Association for the Advancement of the Interests of Labor, begun in the nineteenth century, functioned until 1928, when it was absorbed into the Division of Industrial Relations of the National Council of the Church. The Church Socialist League was begun in 1911, to be superceded by the Church League for Industrial Democracy in 1919. In 1913 the General Convention of the church stated unequivocally that "the Church stands for the ideal of social justice . . . in which . . . every worker shall have a just return for that which he produces, a free opportunity for self-development, and a fair share in all the gains of progress."

The Depression clearly showed the need for social action, and during the 1930s socialism, as well as pacifism, had powerful appeal for Episcopalians. To be sure, there were well-to-do Episcopalians who were complacent and indifferent—some of them were caricatured by such writers as Upton Sinclair. And many Episcopalians were simply caught up in their own struggle for economic survival. But a great many felt a renewed sense of social mission in the country's economic crisis.

The Church League for Industrial Democracy (later called the Episcopal League for Social Action) was especially effective. Many bishops took part in the movement, and the House of Bishops in 1933 issued the "Davenport Pastoral" calling for a cooperative industrial order and the renunciation of war. This active spirit continued through the 1930s, and in 1940 one bishop expressed the thoughts of many in his criticism of a "social order which expresses . . . the selfishness and blindness of the human heart, . . . which puts emphasis on wealth and power, and consecrates the sin of avarice."

World War II, as we have seen, largely put an end to the pacifist movement. During the postwar years, growing antagonism toward the Soviet Union also made socialism unpopular in the country. But the Episcopal church's sense of social mission, once stirred, did not die away.

With all that was happening around it in the twentieth century, the church itself had to change. To begin with, the old *Book of Common Prayer*, which had undergone only minor revision since 1789, needed to be completely rewritten in light of modern learning. Accordingly, the General Convention of 1913 named a commission to undertake the task. Finished in 1928, the resulting prayerbook successfully met the needs of the church for over fifty years. To go with the new prayerbook, the *Hymnal* was revised in 1916, and again in 1940.

Although the introduction of provinces helped in the organization of the church, it soon became clear that a more effective central administration would be needed.

Since the beginning of the Episcopal church, the senior ranking bishop had been designated the presiding bishop of the church and had served as the chief administrative officer. In practice, this meant that bishops did not reach the post until late in life and often retained it after they had ceased to be effective. Accordingly, the General Convention of 1919 established that the office of presiding bishop should be elective. That convention also called for the creation of a National Council for the Church—subsequently called the Executive Council—to act as a central administrative body between conventions.

One of the most important developments within the church in the early twentieth century was the interest in ecumenism. In a way, the Episcopal church had begun the Anglican movement toward ecumenism when its General Convention, meeting in Chicago in 1886, established four points on which the church should base any unification effort. Approved at the Lambeth Conference two years later, this so-called Chicago Quadrilateral became the well known Lambeth Quadrilateral—with its call for unification based on the Bible, the creeds, the sacraments, and the historic episcopate.

Operating on these principles, the Episcopal church has had serious discussions on merger with the Congregationalists, the Presbyterians, the Methodists, and the United Church of Christ. The fourth point in the Lambeth Quadrilateral, however, has often been a stumbling block since these churches either no longer have bishops, or select them independently of the historic line.

But the Episcopal church does maintain official ties

with other churches. It has long been a member of the National Council of the Churches of Christ in the United States and of the World Council of Churches. Henry Knox Sherrill, presiding bishop of the church from 1947 to 1958, served as president of both organizations. The church also maintains close relations with its sister churches in the Anglican Communion, and it remains on friendly terms with the Eastern Orthodox churches.

A kind of high point for the Anglican Communion was the last Anglican Congress, held in Toronto in 1963, drawing elected representatives of the forty-four million baptized Anglicans around the world. This period was also a high point for the Episcopal church. Many of its immediate problems had been overcome and by 1966 it had a membership of 3.6 million, 2.2 million of whom were active communicants. Beginning in that year, however, a slow but steady decline set in, and the church found itself faced with an entirely new set of challenges.

X

New Challenges,
New Directions

WE HAVE SEEN THE EPISCOPAL CHURCH, IN THE COURSE OF
its history, grow as an institution. That institution is
ever changing. As the church entered the last decades
of the twentieth century, it faced a series of new challenges and responded by moving in radically new di-
rections: in its ministry, in its membership, in its
services, and in its very spirit. To some observers it
seems that the Episcopal church we have been describing will soon be no more. In its place will be a new and
very different body. But the church has undergone
great changes in the past and still managed to retain its
essential character. Can it do so again? Only time will
tell.

At mid-century the church was staid, complacent, comfortable, and self-satisfied—hardly a dynamic force in the spiritual life of America. Nor was it a potent social force. Its members were mainly well-to-do and in the mainstream of American life. The Christian socialism and active evangelism of earlier decades was all but forgotten.

The coming decades saw America's conscience stirred. It was a time of social and political activism. In the 1960s the country became engaged in an increasingly unpopular war in Vietnam. Like others, Episcopalians fought in the war, Episcopalians refused to fight in the war, and Episcopalians protested against the war. In the midst of it all, one Episcopalian minister, with President Lyndon Johnson in attendance in his church, delivered a sermon quietly questioning the country's involvement. Although this provoked some negative public response—the minister's own vestry apologized to the president—it was credited by others with prompting a turning point in the president's thinking on the war.

In the 1980s, the country's support of the Contras in Nicaragua was equally divisive. And in the meantime, against the backdrop of the cold war and the nuclear threat, there were repeated crises in the Middle East and concern over American hostages, first in Iran, then in Lebanon.

Moreover, a whole range of social issues troubled American society—from abortion to enthanasia, from ozone depletion and acid rain to obscene rock lyrics. But in the Episcopal church the social issues that came closest to home were the civil rights movement, the women's rights movement, and the drive for gay rights.

By the 1960s the Episcopal church considered itself integrated. There were black church members, black priests, and black bishops. In fact, the integration was largely token. Only about 3.5 percent of the church membership was black, black priests were few, and the only blacks in the episcopacy were suffragan (assistant) bishops or missionary bishops to countries with black populations. Still, the church was not indifferent to the problems of blacks nationwide. In 1967 the General Convention, at the request of the presiding bishop, embarked on a special program to provide up to a million dollars a year for funding minority community organizations.

The more militant black leaders were not satisfied. In 1969 James Foreman marched to the Episcopal Church Center in New York with a staggering list of demands: an immediate payment of $60 million to black leaders, along with a yearly assessment of 60 percent of all profits on church assets, and a full accounting to blacks of all assets of the church in every locality in the country. Unsure how to respond to such extreme demands, church leaders called a special convention which voted a fund of $200,000 for black clergy to dispense to the black population.

Within the church a backlash had begun soon after the institution of the special program in 1967. It now grew to massive proportions. Rather than submit to what they considered extortion by the black militants, many Episcopalians withheld funds from the national church. Others, who saw support of black radical extremists as a sign of dangerous liberal movements within the church, left the church altogether.

The Episcopal church was thus prohibited by its own

membership from associating itself with the militant wing of the black movement. At the same time, however, the church moved steadily toward integration of its membership. The first black diocesan bishop for the United States was elected in Massachusetts in 1970. And a black president of the House of Deputies was elected in 1979. By 1980 it was estimated that there were some 350 black clergymen in the church. Though many of them served the four hundred predominantly black congregations, a number worked in white parishes.

Hispanics, too, were entering the priesthood in larger numbers. In part this was because of the large number of missionary dioceses in Spanish-speaking areas of the world. But the General Convention of 1979 also voted to increase the Hispanic ministry of the church.

Nor has the church abandoned its social concern. In 1980 the Episcopal Urban Caucus was formed, and in 1982 the General Convention's Commission on the Church in Metropolitan Areas began a program to form Jubilee Centers to aid "the poor, the powerless, the vulnerable." By 1985 there were forty such centers.

For years, many—if not most—of the women in the church seemed happy with their secondary, though special role. They sang in the choir, decorated the altar, sewed and repaired vestments, organized rummage sales and church suppers, and raised money for missions. That they rarely served on vestries, could not act as deputies to the General Convention, and could rise in the priesthood no higher than to deaconess did not seem to trouble them.

Other women, however, felt that this subsidiary role

was restrictive and unsatisfying. They saw themselves as equal children of God with men, and some of them felt called to the priesthood. The women's movement affected the Episcopal church as it did the country at large. After some agitation in the 1960s, deaconesses became known simply as deacons, like their male colleagues, and in 1970 women deputies were seated at the General Convention. Yet, the General Convention of 1973 refused, for a second time, to accept the ordination of women to the priesthood.

Those women who felt a call to the priesthood found the situation unacceptable, and a number of the bishops of the church supported their position. Finally, three bishops agreed to ordain women candidates without the approval of the church as a whole. In 1974 they ordained eleven women in Philadelphia.

The ordinations were irregular (outside the usual pattern of ordinations) but not necessarily invalid, since the bishops had the authority to ordain and had followed the accepted forms. Yet, the House of Bishops met almost at once and ruled the ordinations invalid. This action was not binding on the church, however, and only the General Convention could finally decide. In 1976 it ruled that there was no bar to the ordination of women. By 1990 some fourteen hundred women had been ordained.

Many in the church were unhappy with this course of events. Even the presiding bishop indicated that he himself could not accept women as valid priests. Nor was the dissatisfaction limited to men. A great many women were distressed at the new roles opened up for women in the church. An indication of this feeling was the continued existence of the body known as the Episcopal Church Women. Since women were no longer barred from any role in the church, there was no need for them to maintain a separate organization of their own. In fact, the Episcopal Church Women's meeting voted to oppose the Equal Rights Amendment in 1979 at the very time that the General Convention of the church was voting to support it. Clearly, then, there was a real split between the women in the church, some wishing to maintain their old position, others wanting to move to full equality with men.

But the church as a whole was moving toward full equality. Consecration of a woman bishop was to be the next momentous step. The act would have important consequences not only within the Anglican Communion but also for its ecumenical relations, especially with the Roman Catholic and Eastern Orthodox churches. In 1988 the General Convention eased the way for women bishops by allowing future parishes in dioceses with a woman bishop to invite an alternate, male, visiting bishop to preside at baptisms and confirmations if they wished to do so. Later in that year, the monumental step was taken, when the first woman bishop (coincidentally also divorced and a black), Barbara Harris, was elected in Massachusetts. After much controversy, she was approved by the requisite number of dioceses, and was consecrated in February 1989.

The gay rights movement also had its impact on the church, with controversy centering on the ordination of homosexuals as clergy. For many years it had been thought that a number of Episcopalian priests and some bishops were privately homosexual. In 1977, a young woman who had publicly admitted to being a homosexual was ordained by Bishop Paul Moore of New York. There was a storm of protest within the church. But in line with the national movement for gay rights, gay activists rallied in support of the woman. And several other Episcopalian priests, men and women, openly declared their homosexuality. Gay activists hoped to make the ordination of admitted homosexuals an accepted practice within the church. A group of them formed Integrity, an organization working for gay rights within the church.

The matter came before the General Convention of 1979, which voted to recommend that practising homosexuals not be ordained. Following the vote, twenty-three bishops signed a statement indicating that they could not in conscience follow the recommendation and would continue the ordination of worthy homosexuals. To many observers the action of the General Convention was reminiscent of its earlier stand against the ordination of women, a decision certain to be reversed in time.

But the controversy continued through the 1980s. Gay rights advocates won some victories. Bishop Spong of Newark joined Bishop Moore in support of the ordination of gays. In 1985, Bishop Edmond L. Browning, an advocate of gay rights, was elected presiding bishop of the church. In 1989 Bishop Spong's popular book, *Living in Sin?*, proposed a church blessing for committed homosexual couples and unmarried bisexual ones. At the same time, an educational unit of the church prepared a study pamphlet, *Sexuality: A Divine Gift*, which presented quite liberal views on sexual activity outside of marriage, including homosexuality. Also in 1989, Bishop Spong ordained a practicing homosexual, J. Robert Williams. During this time the AIDS epidemic produced much sympathy for gays (and all sufferers of the disease). The presiding bishop supported the Episcopal AIDS Coalition. Among its activities, the coalition contributed a memorial panel to the quilt made in memory of AIDS victims, with names of two hundred Episcopalians who had died of the disease.

But there was powerful resistance to all this. The church's pamphlet was widely condemned, as was Bishop Spong's book. The Reverend Williams was forced to resign his ministry. By the end of the decade, the church as a body had not endorsed the blessing of gay or other unwed couples, nor had it approved the ordination of active gays. Indeed some fundamentalists considered the AIDS epidemic a judgment of God on its victims. Still, many hoped the seeds of tolerance had been planted in the church, seeds that someday, in a better climate, would sprout.

The world-wide radical theology movement of the 1960s made its way into the Episcopal church, most noticeably in the preaching and writing of James Pike, bishop of California. Bishop Pike was accused of heresy for allegedly denying the Virgin Birth and incarnation of Jesus, as well as the three-fold nature of God. No heresy trial was held, but Bishop Pike ultimately did resign his bishopric. Many in the church undoubtedly shared his liberal theological views, but in the 1960s the church was not ready to endorse them publicly.

Social activism in the 1960s and 1970s was manifested in urban riots, civil rights marches, war protests, and demonstrations for women's liberation. There was a temptation for many clergy to express their social concern primarily in these terms. Other clergy became caught up in the group psychology movements which were popular at the time, and various kinds of *encounter groups* were introduced into the life of some parishes.

Changes were also forthcoming in church services, and in the minister's role in those services. Following the like movement in the Church of England, there was a general shift from morning prayer to Holy Communion—now termed the *Eucharist*—as the chief form of Sunday worship. Services were recast to give the laity a more prominent role: reading the lessons from the Bible, leading the prayers of intercession, and administering the sacramental bread and wine at Communion. These changes finally necessitated a further revision of the prayerbook. However, the drastically altered document which was introduced provisionally at the General Convention of 1976, proved highly controversial.

This was the first prayerbook revision since 1928 and the most dramatic since the formulation of the Episcopal *Book of Common Prayer* in 1789. The most significant feature of the new prayerbook was its presentation of all services in two forms, "Rite One" and "Rite Two." For each service, "Rite One" continued with only minor modification the language used in the past. The "Rite Two" services, however, were almost completely altered. Their language had been totally modernized. The "thee" and "thou" of the past had been replaced with "you," and the poetic diction of old had given way to the flat statement of contemporary speech. A comparison of the familiar Lord's Prayer in the two versions (although "Rite Two" allows either form) gives an idea of the changes:

The Lord's Prayer
Rite One

Our Father, who art in heaven,
hallowed by thy Name,
thy kingdom come,
thy will be done,
on earth as it is in heaven.
Give us this day our daily bread.
And forgive us our trespasses,
as we forgive those
who trespass against us.
And lead us not into temptation,
but deliver us from evil.
For thine is the kingdom,
and the power, and the glory,
for ever and ever. Amen.

The Lord's Prayer
Rite Two

Our Father in heaven,
hallowed by your Name,
your kingdom come,
your will be done,
on earth as in heaven.
Give us today our daily bread.
Forgive us our sins
as we forgive those
who sin against us.
Save us from the time of trial,
and deliver us from evil.
For the kingdom, the power,
and the glory are yours,
now and for ever. Amen.

There is no doubt that the new language greatly altered the flavor of the services of the church. The reverent grandeur of the old services had been replaced by the bland cheerfulness of the new. To those who had grown up with the old prayers, the new ones were an outrage, and a great public outcry followed the introduction of the new book.

Still, sentiment within the church soon moved to favor the new prayerbook. When it came up for final approval at the General Convention of 1979, both houses voted for it with hardly a dissenting voice.

This may not be the end of changes in the prayerbook. There is considerable feeling on the part of women activists that all references to God indicating a

masculine gender ought to be changed—that we should
no longer pray to God the "father" or refer to God as
"he." While some would propose giving God feminine
attributes, at least in some circumstances, others would
prefer more neutral formulations, employing what is
termed inclusive language—"God the creator," for instance. The General Convention of 1985 instructed the
church's liturgical commission to develop inclusive-
language liturgies, and the 1988 General Convention
voted that the new services should immediately be
tested in parishes.

While the church was considering these changes in
its ministry and in the prayerbook, it was also undergoing changes of another sort. Something like a new spirit
seemed to infuse the church, activating it much as the
Great Awakening had done in the eighteenth century
and evangelical fervor had in the nineteenth. This spirit
took two forms—a resurgence of evangelism, and the
sudden appearance of Pentacostalism, or *spirit baptism*, one of the chief signs of which is speaking in
tongues.

From the 1960s evangelism had shown new strength
throughout the world, primarily in the fundamentalist
Christian sects and in the enormously popular radio
and television programs of media evangelists. But
Evangelicals became increasingly prominent within
the older churches, too.

In the Episcopal church, the Fellowship of Witness, a
branch of a wider Evangelical fellowship in the Anglican Communion, was founded in 1965. This group
was a force behind the founding of an Evangelical seminary, the Trinity Episcopal School for Ministry in Am-

bridge, Pennsylvania, in 1976. The church hosted ever more Evangelical conferences, workshops, and retreats—brief but intensive conferences at isolated locations. A group known as Faith Alive brought "renewal weekends" to parishes, at which the whole congregation devotes their time to Christian study and prayer. And the Cursillo movement, which began in the Catholic church, organized regular weekend retreats of Christian prayer and teaching. By 1977 the church had set up a national Office of Evangelism and Renewal, and local dioceses and parishes were increasing their efforts at evangelism.

Allied with the Evangelical movement in the church were certain experiments in community living—akin to Christian communes. Like the Evangelicals, these groups focused on spreading the gospel and working for the salvation of others. They were distinctive in that they consisted of individuals, couples, even families, who came together to make a common life devoted to their Christian effort. One of the best known was associated with the Church of the Redeemer in Houston, Texas.

Perhaps the most surprising of all the recent developments in the Episcopal church was the sudden outbreak of Pentecostal, or *Charismatic*, fervor. In 1959, an Episcopal priest in Van Nuys, California, the Reverend Dennis Bennett, underwent the spirit baptism and began speaking in tongues. He encouraged the formation of a Charismatic group in his parish. A year later, though, when he publicly reported on his activities to his congregation, their disapproval and that of his bishop forced his resignation from the parish. Another, more sympathetic bishop invited him to take over a small mission church in Seattle. There he continued his Pentecostal work—very successfully. The congregation grew tenfold, from two hundred to two thousand, in a few years.

Although the new Pentecostal movement was initially condemned by many with authority in the Episcopal church, it later became quite respectable, attracting a number of clergy and laymen. In 1973 the national Episcopal Charismatic Fellowship was founded in Dallas, Texas, and many parishes had active Charismatic groups.

Both Evangelicals and Charismatics brought great enthusiasm to their religious experience. They provided vitality and excitement to the Episcopal church. At the same time, many of those who had been born again or who had experienced spirit baptism looked down on those who had not shared their experiences and considered them less than full Christians. For some, too, these special experiences became an end in themselves, and they turned away from evangelism and social concern. Many old-line Episcopalians, who had been active in their church for many years, resented the enthusiasm and especially the exclusiveness of the newcomers. Hence, the new movements were a source of some division within the Episcopal church.

In line with other changes in the Episcopal church, it has recently become involved in a new kind of ecumenism. Earlier ecumenical efforts, as we have seen, had been on a large scale, seeking complete union of churches. The Episcopal church continues such efforts, and currently participates in the Consultation on

Church Union with nine other Protestant churches. But there is a growing recognition that Christian churches can cooperate without merging. The on-going work of the National and the World Council of Churches are indications of this. And the international Anglican-Roman Catholic consultation has produced doctrinal statements which, it seems, both bodies can accept.

More recently, though, a radically new grass-roots move toward ecumenism has appeared, a tendency for individuals, even parishes, to blur the distinctions between churches and work together at the local level. Protestants have long attended one another's services, even taken Communion at one another's churches. But now the actual merger of local churches has been taking place. In 1990, for instance, a Pentecostal congregation in Georgia merged with the local parish of the Episcopal church.

Episcopalians and Roman Catholics are doing much the same thing, even without the sanction of their churches. In some localities, Episcopal and Roman Catholic parishes—in one case, a whole diocese—have undertaken covenants (made formal vows) to work, study, and pray together to learn more of each other's beliefs and forms of worship.

In fact, the kinds of changes we have seen taking place in the Episcopal church have their counterparts in other denominations. In many ways, as we have noted, the Christian churches are becoming more and more alike, and this would seem to augur well for their future unification.

All of the recent, dramatic changes in the church have provoked some measure of negative response. A number of Episcopalians believe, for example, that in moving toward other churches, the Episcopal church is losing its own identity. Many more Episcopalians, including a former presiding bishop, are unhappy at changes in the ministry, particularly the ordination of women. Their image of a priest is not one they can lightly change. Many, too, are deeply unhappy at changes in the language of the prayerbook and the nature of church services. Without its familiar services, they feel, the Episcopal church cannot be the same.

Some Episcopalians are unhappy but remain loyal to their church. Some, however, have stopped attending services or have joined other denominations. In the 1970s, one group took the extreme step of forming their own, schismatic church, called the Anglican Catholic church (for a short time, the Anglican Church of North America). The new church was founded after the General Convention of 1976 had accepted the new prayerbook and agreed to the ordination of women, the two most troublesome points at issue. Its first, organizational meeting, held in St. Louis in 1977, included some twenty-five hundred bishops, priests, and laymen. Several years later some thirty-five hundred laymen, nearly eighty priests, and four bishops had joined the new church, forming three dozen congregations. Compared to the 2.5 million Episcopalians in 7,500 congregations, these are very small numbers, but the fact that it has four bishops means that the church can maintain itself as an independent body. In fact, the number of persons involved is not very different from those who banded together two hundred years ago to form the Episcopal church.

And as changes in the church continued in the

1980s, so did the opposition. The consecration of the first woman bishop provoked a predictable outcry. Some eighteen hundred who protested the action, including six active and twenty retired bishops, met later the same year in Fort Worth, Texas, to form an organization to combat the changes—most notably the ordination of women and use of the new prayerbook. Calling itself the Episcopal Synod of America, the new group considered separating from the church but chose instead to work within it. The presiding bishop, the Most Reverend Edmond Browning, responded mildly to formation of the group and urged them to remain with the church "for the health of the whole body."

In spite of the negative reactions of some Episcopalians to the changes that the church is undergoing, it would be a mistake to conclude that the church is in serious trouble—or that it is leaving its people behind. Most Episcopalians endorse the changes that are taking place. The actions of recent General Conventions alone suggest that this is the case. A Gallup poll of the church's membership, commissioned by the presiding bishop in 1988, confirmed that large majorities favored the ordination of women bishops but disapproved sanctioning of homosexual unions. (Opinion was divided on the use of non-sexist language in the liturgy.)

The Episcopal church is a corporate body. Its members act together to exercise their common will—inspired, they believe, by the Holy Spirit. Thus, what the church is doing, the way it is moving, is a joint action of the church body. The church cannot leave its people behind. It is its people.

The Episcopal church is changing, most Episcopalians believe, because the world is changing. Though many of its concerns are of the next world, the Episcopal church operates in this world. It must adapt to changes in the world if its work is to be successful. If Episcopalians are coming to think differently about their relations with other churches, if they are beginning to see their priests in new ways, if they are finding new ways to worship their God, that is not surprising. The world of Jesus and the Apostles is no more. The world of Henry VIII and Thomas Cranmer is no more. Even the world of Bishops Seabury and White would not be recognizable today. As the world changes, so must human institutions change—even ones with divine connections.

Thus, to most Episcopalians, it is fitting that the Episcopal church should change. What is important is that the heritage of the past not be lost, that the church move forward in full recognition of where it has been. If the Episcopal church is acquiring a new face, it is still the church of the Apostles, the church of Thomas Cranmer, and the church of Bishop Seabury. It must remain so as long as it is the Episcopal church.

XI

The Structure of the Church

THE EPISCOPAL CHURCH IS, AFTER ALL, AN INSTITUTION, and it is as an institution that it does its work in the world.

To begin with the ministry, the Episcopal church continues the ancient division of the clergy into three orders: deacons, priests (or ministers), and bishops. The Bible alludes to all three classes, and it seems likely that they emerged as separate orders while the Apostles were first organizing the church.

St. Stephen is recorded in the Bible as being the first deacon. It appears that the intent in creating deacons was to provide a kind of assistant priest, for the deacons are described as waiting on tables and distributing alms to the poor, but they were also entrusted with preaching. Indeed, St. Stephen became the first Christian martyr when he was stoned to death while preaching.

Today deacons are an established part of the church. All who enter the ministry are required to serve first as deacons. Although nominally the minimum term is one year, this can be shortened at the discretion of the bishop, and six months is a more usual period. There are also those who serve the church more or less permanently as deacons.

Deacons traditionally assist in baptism, read the gospel during services, administer the chalice at Holy Communion, and dismiss the parishioners at the end of the service. They also visit the sick and infirm, taking the sacrament to those who wish to receive it. When authorized by the bishop, they preach. In parishes that do not have a regular minister, many of the responsibilities can be carried out by a deacon.

The Bible speaks specifically of deaconesses, and there are other records of deaconesses in the early church. By the Middle Ages, however, the practice of naming women deacons had stopped. In the nineteenth century, both the Church of England and the Episcopal church revived the practice, though the order of deaconesses was considered separate from deacons. In the 1960s that distinction was dropped in the Episcopal church (and more recently in the English church), and now both women and men become simply deacons.

The New Testament uses the terms *bishop* (in Greek, *episkopos*, meaning overseer) and *priest* (in Greek, *presbyteros*, meaning elder) almost interchangeably. Both terms were applied to leading members of the early Christian groups. As congregations grew in size and number it became convenient to organize them into larger units called dioceses. The term *bishop* was then reserved for the person with oversight over the diocese, while the person who led the congregation was the *presbyter* or *priest*. Over the centuries this distinction was confirmed and two separate orders of clergy were recognized.

In the Episcopal church today, as in the other churches of the Anglican Communion, the individual priests are chiefly the spiritual heads of their congregations. They conduct the services, and only they can consecrate the bread and wine at Holy Communion. Only they give absolution to those who confess their sins. They are also responsible for making the church a center for the life of the congregation. In their various activities, priests are assisted by lay members of their congregation, especially in managing the financial affairs of the parish. In large parishes, also, assistant priests may aid in various activities, and parish ministry is increasingly a group responsibility.

Candidates for the priesthood feel a special call to serve in the ministry. Upon the recommendation of their parish priest, they usually attend a seminary for three years, undergo an examination, and are then ordained, first as a deacon, finally as a priest. The priesthood was officially opened to women at the General Convention of 1976, and by 1990 some fourteen hundred women had been ordained as priests.

All three orders of ministers in the Episcopal church are free to marry, but some individuals prefer to remain single, especially those in religious orders.

The exact role and title of the clergy vary from parish

to parish. In some, high church congregations, they are thought of particularly as priests, who celebrate the Mass. In such parishes the priest is likely to be called "Father _____." (There seems to be no comparable term for women priests.) In low church parishes the clergy are more frequently referred to as ministers or rectors and the service is Holy Communion. The term *Eucharist* is now in common use. Rectors in these parishes are referred to as "the Reverend Mr. _____," "the Reverend Mrs. _____," or "the Reverend Miss _____." Sometimes, simply, "Mr. _____," "Mrs. _____," or "Miss _____." The adjective form "the Reverend _____" is sometimes mistaken for a title, and the form "Reverend _____" is used. But this is technically incorrect.

The bishops in the Episcopal church can perform all the same functions as deacons and priests, but they also have specific duties of their own. They perform the rite of confirmation, in which each church member renews the vows made on his behalf at baptism. They also ordain deacons and priests. Both confirmation and ordination are accomplished by the *laying on of hands*, a ceremony in which the bishop presses his hands on the head of the person being confirmed or ordained.

The church in which the bishop regularly conducts services is the cathedral. There is one for each diocese. He also travels around the diocese periodically, visiting local parishes, participating in services, and conducting confirmations. There is one chief bishop for each diocese—the diocesan bishop—and he is the primary administrator. But there may be one or more assistant bishops in various categories. A bishop coadjutor is an assistant for the whole diocese, who automatically succeeds the diocesan bishop when he dies or is unable to continue in office. A suffragan bishop is an assistant bishop assigned to a particular city or area within a diocese.

Any priest in the church can become a bishop. This now includes women. The key step in selection of a new bishop is a diocesan convention called for that purpose. Usually a nominating committee proposes one or more leading candidates and other names are taken from the floor. The winning candidate must be approved by a majority of the other bishops and diocesan conventions. Finally, the candidate is ordained and consecrated by at least three other bishops, one of whom is the presiding bishop or a representative. By custom, bishops are referred to as "the Right Reverend _____."

Although other churches in the Anglican Communion have archbishops, like the Church of England, the Episcopal church does not. The various provinces into which the dioceses are grouped hold conventions, called synods, at which one of the bishops is elected president, but he is not considered to have authority over other bishops in the province. The presiding bishop, or primate, of the whole church is elected at a General Convention and holds office for only twelve years or until he reaches the age of seventy. He gives up his seat as diocesan bishop when he becomes chief administrator of the church. In his relations with the other bishops he is considered rather "first among equals" than a superior. He is often referred to as "the Most Reverend _____."[7] The National Cathedral in Washington, D.C., is his official seat.

Lay persons also play a role in the ministry of the

Episcopal church. In a sense, every member of the church shares its ministry and acts for the church in his or her daily life. More formally, some are designated lay readers, persons authorized to read sermons, offer the daily office of prayers, and visit the sick. In small congregations without ministers of their own, lay readers can perform many of the priestly functions. Moreover, laymen function at every level of the administration of the church.

The smallest administrative unit in the church is the individual parish. Conducting the business of the parish is an elected vestry of nine to fifteen men and women, who come together—usually monthly—in a meeting chaired by the rector. Headed by a junior and senior warden, the vestry is responsible for the financial and legal affairs of the parish. It also conducts the search for a new rector when the post is vacant. Parishes may have a full- or part-time lay secretary, and many have councils or other committees to aid in parish work. Various clubs and other organizations associated with the parish meet regularly for charitable, educational, or merely social purposes.

A clergyman called to a parish serves as rector for an indefinite time. He or she is not an employee of the congregation but a professional person carrying out his or her ministry in the parish. Large parishes have one or more curates, assistants to the rector, who can be priests or deacons.

Most parishes are self-supporting and in fact contribute to the diocese and the national church. Some that are small or in poorer areas receive a subsidy from the diocese. Known as missions, such parishes are headed by a priest appointed by the bishop.

The parishes and missions in an area are organized, as we have seen, into a larger unit, the diocese. An annual diocesan convention, headed by the bishop, conducts the affairs of the diocese. It also elects bishops when there are vacancies and appoints committees and councils to fulfill various functions. The most important of these, the so-called standing committee, approves candidates for the ministry, votes on bishops elected by other dioceses, and runs the diocese when the office of bishop is vacant. All clergy participate in the diocesan convention, and lay delegates are elected by local vestries and congregations.

The dioceses themselves are grouped into the nine provinces: New England, New York and New Jersey, Washington (the Mid-Atlantic), Sewanee (the Southeast), the Midwest, the Northwest, the Southwest, the Pacific (the West Coast, Alaska, Hawaii, and Taiwan), and the Caribbean (Mexico and Central America). The periodic synods of each province give the member dioceses a chance to meet and discuss common problems, but the provinces do not play a major role in national church administration.

The body that charts the overall course of the church is the General Convention. Meeting every three years, more frequently if necessary, the General Convention consists of two houses, the House of Bishops and the House of Deputies. All bishops meet in the House of Bishops. The House of Deputies includes four clergy and four lay deputies from each diocese. Since 1970 women deputies have been admitted. Besides electing the presiding bishop, who serves as its chair, the House of Bishops chooses a vice chairman and a secretary. The deputies elect a president, vice president, and secretary, and *concur* in the election of the presiding bishop. All resolutions must pass both houses, and on matters of importance the House of Deputies vote *by orders*, with the clergy and lay deputies voting separately.

The General Convention is the final decision-making body in the church. Working largely through committees, it decides the general business of the church, setting budgets, making constitutional and canonical changes, and determining matters relating to missions.

A separate organization for women in the church, the Episcopal Church Women, meets every three years alongside the General Convention. Although this organization is not an official part of the church structure, it is nonetheless influential.

Between General Conventions, a number of standing committees meet regularly, preparing matters for consideration at the next convention. Most importantly, the executive council implements policy established by previous conventions. It meets three or four times a year. Headed by the presiding bishop, the executive council consists of one lay and one clerical representative from each of the nine provinces, plus four bishops, four clergy, and twelve lay members elected at the General Convention to staggered six-year terms. The council also operates through standing committees, which oversee the church's activities in a number of areas: finance, communication, development, education, and missionary work at home and abroad. From time to time, the House of Bishops meets between conventions to advise the presiding bishop on matters of immediate concern.

To handle the day-to-day business of the church, a

permanent administrative office is maintained at the Episcopal Church Center in New York City. It has administrative divisions corresponding to the varied activities of the national church. Its staff members work closely with the executive council.

In addition, there are a number of official agencies of the church. The Church Pension Fund was established in 1917 to help meet the needs of retired clergy. Allied with it are the Church Insurance Companies which insure the lives of clergy and the property of parishes. The Church Building Fund assists in the construction and repair of churches and rectories. The Church Historical Society maintains the church archives, fosters research in church history, and publishes a quarterly *Historical Magazine*. A monthly newspaper devoted to church news, the *Episcopalian* is independently edited but sponsored by the church. The church also publishes *Forward Day by Day*, a set of daily devotional readings, as well as other devotional pamphlets and books. The church publishes its own *Hymnal* and the *Book of Common Prayer*.

Like other religious denominations, the Episcopal Church has a number of seminaries to train individuals for the ministry. In addition to the General Theological Seminary in New York City, the church has more than a dozen seminaries and theological schools around the country. Overseas, it maintains St. Andrew's Theological Seminary in Mexico City, and one of the same name in Manila.

To aid in the education of its own young people and others who care to attend, the church supports the University of the South (Sewanee, Tennessee) and several general colleges, Bard (Annandale-on-Hudson,

New York), Hobart (Geneva, New York), and Kenyon (Gambier, Ohio). It also supports three primarily black colleges, St. Paul's (Lawrenceville, Virginia), Voorhees (Denmark, South Carolina) and St. Augustine's (Raleigh, North Carolina). Since 1980 it has supported St. Augustine College (Chicago, Illinois), a two-year bilingual institution (Spanish-English). Abroad, it sponsors Cuttington University in Liberia and Trinity College in the Philippines.

Episcopalian students, of course, also attend other private and public colleges and universities, and the church has chapels and chaplains for them at most American schools. There are also scores of Episcopal preparatory schools in the country, and many parishes run their own day schools. For the army, navy, and air force, and for the veterans' hospitals, the church maintains dozens of chaplains. Their work is guided by a bishop for the armed forces.

The church also has special ministries to seamen; to alcoholics; and to the blind, the deaf, and the aging. Many dioceses have conference, camp, and retreat centers, and a number have health and welfare agencies, supporting the young, the ill, the aged, and the needy.

People are often surprised to learn that there are religious orders in the Episcopal church. They think of nuns and monks as being only Roman Catholic. In fact there are more than a dozen orders for men and women in the Episcopal church, and nearly a dozen that admit both. Some of them, such as the Benedictines and Franciscans, are much like their Roman Catholic counterparts. Others are uniquely Anglican, American branches of wider Anglican orders. One, which includes both men and women—the Order of the Agape and Reconciliation—is ecumenical. Though Anglican-sponsored, it has Roman Catholic and Eastern Ortho-dox members.

Some of the orders in the Episcopal church are cloistered—that is, members live largely within the walls of their convent or monastery. Usually, people in such orders do not marry, and their lives are dedicated primarily to prayer and contemplation. Those in other orders, however, spend much of their time in the world. They do charitable and educational work in parishes and schools, hospitals, and other institutions. People in some orders are permitted to marry. Only persons in the priesthood may enter some orders. Others are open to laymen.

In addition to the religious orders, there are a number of other organizations for priests and laymen within the church. Most are dedicated to joint worship, Bible reading, study of the church, and works of charity. There are also special associations for blacks, gays, and feminists. Evangelicals, Charismatics, and Anglo-Catholics all have their own organizations within the church, too.

As an institutional structure, then, the Episcopal church is complex. Yet, no mere description of the organization can give an idea of it as a living body. What a church is and does is something more than these practical details alone would suggest. The real spirit of the Episcopal church, like that of any church, lies in what its members believe and practice.

XII

The Beliefs and Practices of the Church

THE BELIEFS OF THE EPISCOPAL CHURCH—LIKE THOSE OF the other Anglican churches—are best summed up in the terms of the Lambeth Quadrilateral, which states the essentials of Anglicanism to be preserved in any union of churches: belief in the Bible, the Apostles' and Nicene Creeds, the sacraments of baptism and Holy Communion, and the historical episcopate.

First, then, the Bible. Episcopalians believe that the Bible was inspired by God and that it contains everything necessary for salvation. But they do not insist that everything in the Bible is to be taken literally. The truth in the Bible, they believe, is often presented in language that was highly expressive in Biblical times, but must be reinterpreted in our own day. Thus, the "seven days" of creation may be only a poetic way of describing the events that brought the universe into being—as vivid to us as it was to those who first heard it thousands of years ago, but no longer meaning quite the same thing.

A characteristic of the Episcopal church services is extensive reading from the Bible. During daily morning prayer for example, the entire Bible is read through in two years. Typically, Episcopal churches use some edition of the King James Version. For years the edition most widely used was the Revised Standard Version, which was developed jointly with other American Protestant churches. It is modernized, yet was intended by its makers to preserve "those qualities which have given to the King James Version, a supreme place in English literature." More recently, other, more radically modernized editions have been used in many churches, and in 1990 a New Revised Standard Version was issued, which departs considerably from the old language.

Episcopalians affirm their beliefs during services by reciting the Apostles' or the Nicene Creed. The Apostles' Creed, slightly the simpler of the two, reads (in its new version) as follows:

> I believe in God, the Father almighty, Creator of heaven and earth. I believe in Jesus Christ, his only Son, our Lord. He was conceived by the power of the Holy Spirit and born of the Virgin Mary. He suffered under Pontius Pilate, was crucified, died, and was buried. He descended to the dead. On the third day he rose again. He

ascended into heaven, and is seated at the right hand of the Father. He will come again to judge the living and the dead. I believe in the Holy Spirit, the holy catholic Church, the communion of saints, the forgiveness of sins, the resurrection of the body, and the life everlasting. Amen.

The most significant beliefs specifically referred to in the creed are the following: that God exists in Three Persons, namely the Father, Son (Jesus Christ), and Holy Spirit; that Jesus was born of a virgin, was crucified, died, and then, on the third day, "ascended into heaven"; that the church is universal (catholic); that sins can be forgiven; and that the soul is immortal.

The church offers no detailed interpretation of the various statements in the creeds, and Episcopalians differ widely in what they make of them. Some see the supernatural aspects of these beliefs as literal assertions of the miraculous actions of God. Others view them as poetic expression of difficult-to-understand truths, which it would be impossible to describe in other terms. For instance, in what sense is Jesus the *Son of God?* Episcopalians would answer the question in different ways. Some would say that he is a biological son, others a spiritual son. But all would agree that the relationship must be a special one if the word *son* is used at all.

A fuller statement of Episcopal beliefs is contained in the Thirty-Nine Articles, slightly modified from those of the Church of England. These articles, which amplify the words of the creeds and deal with other matters, such as the marriage of priests, are officially adopted by the Episcopal church and are printed in the prayerbook. But neither clergy nor laity are required to subscribe to them.

Various ceremonies of the church, including marriage, are sometimes referred to as *sacraments*, but the Lambeth Quadrilateral singles out only two as essential, baptism and Holy Communion. Sacraments, in the words of the catechism (a question and answer introduction to the church found in the prayerbook), are "outward and visible signs of inward and spiritual grace." They are, in effect, ties that strengthen the bonds between God and man.

According to the catechism, baptism is both "union with Christ in his death and resurrection" and "birth into God's family the Church." The symbolism thus involves both death and life, but the emphasis is on rebirth. The ceremony is conducted at a baptismal font, usually a basin of stone or metal mounted on a pedestal. After a number of prayers and vows made by those being baptized or those acting for them, the persons being baptized are partially immersed or water is poured over them. They are then given "Christian" names and pronounced baptized "in the name of the Father, and of the Son, and of the Holy Spirit."

Episcopalians are customarily baptized as infants, but older children and adult converts also are baptized. It might be thought that an infant being baptized has no sense of the promises made on his behalf. Episcopalians believe that this does not prevent the child from receiving God's grace, and his parents or sponsors promise to raise him within the church. Nonetheless, those baptized are given the opportunity to renew their vows at the rite of a confirmation.

Confirmation is carried out after the child has reached a responsible age, usually early adolescence, and has completed a course of instruction about the church. The rite itself features the laying on of hands by the bishop. In the past, persons not confirmed were not admitted to Holy Communion, and young people made their "first Communion" only after they had participated in this role. Now, however, in most parishes everyone who has been baptized receives Communion.

The sacrament of the Holy Eucharist is surely the most important ceremony of the Episcopal church. Lying somewhere between the Protestant Lord's Supper and the Catholic Mass, it is known by either name in particular churches and was for many years commonly referred to as Holy Communion. It is performed in memory of the Last Supper, the final meal Jesus had with his disciples before the Crucifixion.

In the ceremony, the communicants pray together, jointly confess their sins, and receive absolution from the priest. Then they approach the altar, kneel (in some churches, stand), and receive the bread (usually a small wafer) in their hands (or mouth), and sip the wine from a goblet, or chalice. Some people, for reasons of health, prefer to avoid drinking from the common cup, so they hold the wafer and dip it in the wine before eating it, a procedure known as *intinction*.

As in the other Protestant churches, the Eucharist service is an act of fellowship as well as a memorial of the Last Supper. It brings the members of the church together in joint participation in their most important sacrament. It is traditional that Episcopalians take Communion weekly, and to remain an active communicant in the church one is expected to do so at least three times a year.

The idea of commemorating the Last Supper derives from Jesus' words and actions at that time. In the words of the new prayerbook:

> [He] took bread; and when he had given thanks to you, he broke it, and gave it to his disciples, and said, "Take, eat: This is my Body, which is given for you. Do this for the remembrance of me." After supper, he took the cup of wine; and when he had given thanks, he gave it to them, and said, "Drink this, all of you: this is my Blood of the New Covenant which is shed for you and for many for the forgiveness of sins. Whenever you drink it, do this for the remembrance of me."

This scene is in effect reenacted as the sacrament of the Eucharist.

Yet, for many Episcopalians, as for Roman Catholics, the Holy Communion goes beyond fellowship and commemoration. There is a sense of participation in the rite performed by Jesus, a feeling that Jesus himself is present at the sacrament. On two points, though, the Episcopal church stands firm. The Eucharist is not a sacrifice. Christ made the sacrifice; the sacrament is a celebration of it. And the bread and wine are not actually converted into the Body and Blood of Christ (as in the Roman Catholic doctrine of Transubstantiation).

Still, Christ said of the bread and wine, "This is my body. . . . This is my blood. . . ." Thus, the Body and Blood of Christ are presumed to be present in some way during the Communion. To most Episcopalians, perhaps, this presence is thought to be symbolic or metaphoric—the bread and wine symbolize or stand for the Body and Blood. As some have put it, the Body and Blood are present, but in the hearts and minds of the communicants, not in the bread and wine. It is part of the character of the Episcopal church—like other Anglican churches—that various interpretations of the meaning of the Holy Eucharist are equally acceptable.

These various notions of the character of the Eucharist affect the ceremonies that surround it. In low church parishes, which focus on the fellowship in the service, there is little ceremony. The congregation slowly files up, quietly takes Communion from the hands of its minister, and reverently returns to its seat. In high church parishes, in which the sacramental character is emphasized, there is much ceremony. The priest and communicants perform various symbolic actions at particular moments during the Mass, genuflecting (kneeling briefly on one knee), bowing the head, and making the sign of the cross. Robed acolytes often assist the priest.

Although baptism and the Eucharist are the recognized sacraments of the church, there are a number of other important rites, including confirmation; marriage and burial services; ordination and consecration of bishops, priests, and deacons; consecration of new churches; and the installation of ministers into churches. The prayers and ceremonies for all of these are spelled out in the prayerbook. The church discourages private confession of sins, but the practice does occur in some parishes.

The fourth element in the Lambeth Quadrilateral is the historic episcopate. To Episcopalians the apostolic succession is a real and ongoing direct line of descent from the Apostles, with bishops having consecrated bishops in a continuing sequence from the Apostles personally selected by Christ. All priests, too, are ordained by bishops, and Episcopalians feel this gives their ministry its special character.

All members of the Episcopal church are confirmed by bishops, and bishops visit every parish in their diocese, traditionally at least once a year. The bishop's visit is a major event in the parish, signifying its ties with the church at large. Thus, to every Episcopalian, the bishop is an important figure. Indeed, to be an *Episcopalian* means to have a bishop *(episkopos)*.

Christianity is often characterized in terms of *faith* and *works*, that is beliefs and practices. The practices of the Episcopal church, its varieties of activity, can best be summed up as evangelical, social, ecumenical, and liturgical. An Episcopalian is as an Episcopalian does.

Although Episcopalians are often accused of lacking in Evangelical fervor, we have seen that evangelism has been an important part of the Episcopalian heritage. And Episcopalians today, no less than those of the past, are charged with spreading the word of God to their neighbors.

To Cain's question, "Am I my brother's keeper?" Episcopalians traditionally have answered yes. And social action historically has been an important element in the Episcopalian mission in the world. That mission continues today.

Episcopalians also view it as an essential part of their mission to work toward the reunion of the "one, holy, catholic, and apostolic church." Hence, any consideration of Episcopalian practice must take note of ecumenical efforts. Especially today, this includes the efforts of individual Episcopalians in their local parishes to work in close harmony with fellow Christians of all denominations.

But it is its liturgical practice that is so especially characteristic of the Episcopal church. If Episcopalians are charged to do much of their work outside of their churches, it is in coming back within them that their faith and fellowship is rekindled. The services of the church, then, are truly central to its mission in the world.

The regular services of the church, in addition to the Eucharist, are morning and evening prayer. The language for these is specified in the prayerbook. In many churches, services are held during the week, especially during Lent. Sometimes, there are daily services. Invariably, however, the chief day for churchgoing is Sunday, and the late-morning service, at around ten-thirty or eleven o'clock, is the most widely attended. In older, traditional parishes, there will be an early Eucharist service at around eight, followed by morning prayer at ten-thirty, and evening prayer at five or seven. Where this pattern is followed, the ten-thirty service will be the Eucharist one day a month. Often a Sunday school for children is conducted at the same time as the main service for adults.

The more common pattern today is for the main weekly service at ten-thirty or eleven to be the Eucharist. This is held as a family service, with all generations participating together. Usually a church school is held for the children before the Eucharist. Special ser-

vices, folk masses, and Charismatic and healing services are now often held regularly—generally at times
other than the main Sunday morning service, such as
Sunday or weekday nights.

The typical services of the Episcopal church are liturgical, in that they follow a set pattern and make use
of a standard language. The participants reflect on the
meaning and significance of familiar words and actions, rather than trying to devise new ones on the spur
of the moment. At major services, there is a sermon to
instruct and guide the congregation. There have been
many famous preachers in the Episcopal church, such
as Phillips Brooks in the late nineteenth century. Often,
however, the sermon takes second place to the liturgical events. The congregation takes an active part in
the service in many ways, singing hymns, joining in
prayers, giving responses. A general rule is that Episcopalians "kneel to pray, stand to praise, and sit to learn."
Hence, the congregation kneels while it is saying
prayers, stands to say the creed and sing hymns, and
sits during Bible readings and sermons. Charismatic
services tend to be more spontaneous, and the Charismatic movement has brought more liveliness generally
to church services. Healing services feature the laying
on of hands.

Since the Episcopal church has both a Protestant and
a Catholic heritage, its services traditionally have been
a blend of the puritanical and the ceremonial. Some
churches are bare and unadorned and have services
that are simple in the extreme. Others are highly decorated and have services performed with elaborate ceremony. Most lie somewhere in between. The cathedral
resembles a church, but is usually more elaborately
designed and decorated.

Generally the priest wears a narrow black gown called a cassock, with a short, loose, white garment, called a surplice, hanging over it. A colored, scarf-like stole may be added for Communion. In more elaborate Communion services a chasuble, a decorated, sleeveless outer garment constructed like a poncho, is worn. The bishop generally has more elaborate garb and traditionally wears a peaked, divided, brimless hat called a mitre. He or she also wears a ring and carries a staff.

Stained glass windows, altar cloths, flowers and candles, decorated screens behind the altar—all these add color in many churches. Almost always there is an organ, which is played before and after the main service and accompanies hymns and special selections by the choir. Choirs may consist of a small group of neighbors, who simply gather on Sunday mornings to sing the hymns, or a large group of carefully selected people, who work hard and practice with a professional director in order to produce particularly beautiful music. Now rock music and other non-traditional forms are used in some services, and even dancers participate.

Episcopal churches in the past tended either to be narrow stone structures, vaguely Gothic in inspiration, or regular wooden boxes, more Puritan in derivation. They were built on a cruciform pattern, with the altar at the end of the center, short arm. Newer churches, however, usually have a rather broad, open pattern, more like a wheel than a cross. This change in church structure, coupled with the changes in liturgy, has brought a very different feel to services. No longer is the priest a celebrant of the Mass at the altar at the end of the church, far removed from the congregation; nor is he a preacher standing high above them in a pulpit delivering his sermon. Instead the priest is in the midst of the congregation, joining with them in the celebration of the Eucharist and speaking with them rather than to them.

There are those in the church who are fighting to retain the old liturgical patterns and what they take to be the old religious values. But to those congregations which have fully embraced the new ways, they have become familiar and comfortable. The new language has its own meaning, the new ceremonies their own effects. Presumably they will in time become as dear to the hearts of new generations of Episcopalians, as the old words and the old ways were to earlier generations.

Episcopalians have been accused of loving spectacle, and even today their services are said to be theatrical, perhaps operatic. While there is perhaps some truth to that charge, more often the ceremonies are dignified and truly reflect the participants' feelings about their God and their fellow communicants. For most Episcopalians "going to church," particularly on Sunday morning, is the most important part of their spiritual lives, indeed the most important part of their lives.

PART THREE

THE ANGLICAN COMMUNION

XIII

The Worldwide Fellowship of Anglican Churches

IT WOULD BE OF COURSE BUT ONE MORE EXAMPLE OF Anglo-American parochialism to write of the Church of England and the Episcopal Church of the United States as if they were the only examples of Anglicanism. In fact, they now represent neither the largest (in terms of active communicants) nor the strongest—though perhaps they are the most affluent—of the churches of the world-wide Anglican Communion. In fact, the face of the "typical" Anglican today is not Anglo-Saxon, but either African or Asian. It is in Africa that Anglicanism is showing its greatest growth. Estimates indicate that by 1990 there were as many Anglicans in Uganda alone as in the United States, and it has been said that a typical Sunday in England sees more of the minority Roman Catholics in church than it does Anglicans.

Under these circumstances it is perhaps not surprising that the two best-known names associated with Anglicanism in the world in 1990 were Terry Waite, the representative of the archbishop of Canterbury who remained a hostage in the Middle East, and Nobel laureate Desmond Tutu, archbishop of Cape Town and active witness against South African apartheid.

To be sure, the English and the American churches do have their special places in the communion. It is, after all, the see of Canterbury that began the Anglican story and to which all the other Anglican churches are allied. For its part, the American Episcopal church, the eldest of the daughter churches, has done much in the way of missionary work to bring about the birth of the younger churches. Nonetheless, the newcomers have made themselves at home in the Anglican fellowship and are changing its character in many ways—although not however without some strains and disruptions. It is not simply a case of the new against the old; rather, the problems faced by the older churches, situated in their "highly developed" societies, are very different from those of the churches in the "underdeveloped" areas of the world.

The Anglican Communion today is dispersed and diverse—but a fellowship nonetheless. The nature and some of the implications of that diversity are worth exploring.

To begin historically, besides the Church of England and the Episcopal church there is another family of

Anglo-Saxon and Celtic churches. These are the churches of the British Isles—the Churches of Scotland, Ireland, and Wales—and those of the old dominions—Canada, Australia, and New Zealand. The Churches of Scotland, Ireland, and Wales are all disestablished churches (not supported by their governments), and minority churches, but active nonetheless. The Church of Ireland is notably visible in both the Irish Republic and Northern Ireland, where it has not associated itself with the most extremely anti-Catholic elements. In some respects, these are the Anglican churches most like the Church of England.

The Anglican churches of Canada, Australia, and New Zealand resemble rather the Episcopal church of the United States. They are moderately sized but highly visible because of their association with the English church and their historical role in the early development of their countries. They too are churches associated with the "developed" rather than the "developing" world. They are also like the Episcopal church in the strength of their women's movements. While Australia has been more restrained, Canada and New Zealand have already begun the ordination of women as priests. And in 1989 New Zealand's Anglicans joined Episcopalians in the United States in electing a woman bishop.

In the Americas, besides the Episcopal Church of the United States and the Anglican Church of Canada, there are a number of Anglican churches in Central and South America—namely in the West Indies, Brazil (Igreja Episcopal do Brasil), and the Southern Cone of South America (Iglesia Anglicana del Cono Sud de las Americas). More than a dozen dioceses in Mexico and

Central America are in the Caribbean province of the Episcopal Church of the United States. Loosely associated with them are dioceses in Puerto Rico, Venezuela, and Costa Rica. There are also active dioceses in Bermuda and Cuba. Movements are underway toward the formation of other independent churches in Mexico, Central America, and the Caribbean. Many of the modern churches in this area are, of course, the fruits of over a century of missionary work.

Of the Asian churches, the Episcopal Church of Jerusalem and the Middle East is in an especially precarious position, caught in the crossfire between the Arabs and the Jews. Its thirty thousand members live in Israel, as well as Iran, Egypt, Libya, and eight other largely Arab countries. Similarly, the small Church of Sri Lanka finds itself situated in the midst of the troubled religious and political conflicts between warring Tamils and Sinhalese on the island (formerly Ceylon) off the coast of India.

On the Indian subcontinent, the Anglican church has developed in an unusual way. In 1947, as we have seen, the local Anglican church aligned itself with Methodist, Presbyterian, and Congregationalist groups to form the Church of South India. Now there are comparable churches in North India, Pakistan, and Bangladesh. Like the Church of South India, these are not members of the Anglican Communion but are in communion with it.

The status of the Anglican church in mainland China is difficult to assess today. There was an Anglican church in China before the Communist takeover—the Holy Catholic Church (Chung Hua Sheng Kung Hui).

But the Communist government suppressed the regular Western churches and permitted only its own official Christian churches (both Protestant and Catholic). In 1980 it was learned that there were eight Chinese bishops still living, some active in the official church. It is suspected that remnants of the old churches remain as house churches, meeting in secret in members' homes and attempting to retain some semblance of the old church identity.

The flourishing, century-old Holy Catholic Church in Japan (Nippon Seikokai) has sixty thousand members. Though it has long been a member of the Anglican Communion, it was represented for the first time at a Lambeth Conference in 1988. The somewhat smaller Anglican Church of Burma manages to survive in a state which is essentially Buddhist and not at all hospitable to Christianity.

The province of Melanesia, centering on the Solomon Islands, was recognized as a separate church in 1975. It now has some ninety thousand members. The Church of the Province of Papua New Guinea has perhaps twice the membership. In 1988 the Philippine Episcopal church separated from the American Episcopal church, of which it had long been a part, to become the newest member of the Anglican Communion. Finally, a number of Asian Anglican dioceses, not yet organized into full churches, are members of the Council of the Churches in East Asia. Included are dioceses in Korea, Malaysia, Singapore, Hong Kong, and Macao. Dioceses on Taiwan are part of the Pacific province of the Episcopal Church of the United States. Undoubtedly, new provinces of the Anglican Communion will soon be formed in this part of the world.

Even more than in Asia perhaps, it is in Africa that the growth of the Anglican churches is greatest. A great many of the African Anglican churches are based in former British colonies or protectorates. They began as the churches of English colonists, but by virtue of active missionary work drew increasingly on the native populations for membership. Just as the native Africans obtained political control of their own nations while remaining within the British Commonwealth, so the African Anglican churches have achieved their own identity as national churches but remained within the Anglican Communion.

Generally speaking, it is in the southern part of Africa that the Christian churches have found the most favor. The north, on the other hand, has been most heavily penetrated by the Muslims. In between, the populations are divided, and conflict here is frequent, particularly in the light of increasingly militant Islamic fundamentalism. It is on the basis of these two principles—the pattern of English settlement, and tensions between Christians and Muslims—that we can best understand the situation of the African Anglican churches.

South Africa, with its minority white rule and the enforcement of apartheid, is something of an exception, but not dramatically so. For its Anglican church, developing from the church of the English settlers, has not followed the segregationist practices which have only recently been abandoned by the Dutch Reformed churches of the Afrikaners. Thus it is not surprising that the two-million-member Anglican Church of the Province of Southern Africa, encompassing also dioceses in Mozambique, Namibia and the black "homelands" in South Africa, should have a substantial black membership including its archbishop, Desmond Tutu.

Just to the north of South Africa lie the modern states of Botswana, Zimbabwe, Zambia, and Malawi (under British rule, Bechuanaland, Rhodesia, Northern Rhodesia, and Nyasaland, respectively). These states are served by the Church of the Province of Central Africa, with over a half million members.

In the old British East Africa are now the states of Tanzania, Kenya, and Uganda, each with its own independent Anglican church. The churches of Tanzania and Kenya are each over a million strong, while the Church of Uganda has well over two million members (a fourth of the Christians in the country). In this region, however, Muslims are active—representing a third of the population in Tanzania, for instance—and conflicts are common. Off the coast of East Africa, the Church of the Province of the Indian Ocean, situated on the islands of Madagascar (the Malagasy Republic), Mauritius, and the Seychelles, is also a member of the Anglican Communion.

Immediately west of Tanzania and Uganda, in the former Belgian colonies of the Congo region, are Burundi, Rwanda, and Zaire. They form the territory of the French-speaking church of the Province of Burundi, Rwanda, and Zaire, with about two-thirds of a million members. Its somewhat anomalous position can be traced to the work of a heroic Ugandan missionary who, in the early years of the century, carried the gospel into what was then the darkest heart of Africa.

North of Kenya and Uganda is the Sudan, once the Anglo-Egyptian Sudan, now a country wracked by civil war, floods, and drought. The Episcopal Church of Sudan faces considerable animosity from the large Muslim population, and real dangers from the imposition of fundamentalist Islamic law.

Nigeria, on the west coast of Africa, also has a population which is half militant Muslim. This country too is poverty-stricken and undergoing considerable unrest. The four-million-member Church of the Province of Nigeria—second in size only to the Roman Catholic church among the Christian churches there—is facing considerable violence at the hands of Muslim fanatics. Christian churches are burned with some frequency.

Further along the coast is the Church of the Province of West Africa. Its dioceses lie in the former English colonies of Gambia, Ghana, Guinea, and Sierra Leone, as well as in Liberia, the independent country founded in the nineteenth century by freed American slaves. The church has roughly a third of a million members overall.

Thus, the African Anglican churches represent a very large number of communicants. And by all accounts that number is growing rapidly. One diocese in Tanzania alone had established a new congregation every week over a fifteen-year period. It is little wonder that the voice of the African Anglicans is being heard with increasing frequency in the councils of the Anglican Communion.

XIV

Anglican Structures— Anglican Hazards and Hopes

AS THE TWENTY-EIGHT MEMBER CHURCHES OF THE AN-glican Communion attest, the peculiar genius of Anglicanism lies in its native, national churches. Indeed, it is the principle—and practice—of the autonomy of the national church that gave birth to the Church of England during the Reformation. And as Anglicanism has spread around the world, with missionary districts growing, consolidating, and coalescing, what have come into being are not arms or extensions of the Church of England, but as we have seen new indigenous churches, each with its own special character and flavor.

Even as it has put into practice this principle of autonomy, however, Anglicanism has asserted its allegiance to the doctrine of unity, its belief in the "one, holy, catholic, and apostolic church." In separating from the Roman Catholic church, the English church saw itself as simply reaffirming its descent from, and identity with, the apostolic church of the early fathers. Further, as independent Anglican churches have come into being one-by-one, they have claimed fellowship with the Church of England, and have found the symbol of that fellowship in the see of Canterbury, the historic seat of Anglicanism. As that fellowship has grown and as the sense of the Anglican community as an entity in itself has developed, means have had to be found to maintain the ties that sustain it.

Although he is the central symbol that sustains the Anglican Communion, the archbishop of Canterbury is also the head of the English church, the primate of all England. As such he is a political appointee, formally named by the monarch—in fact selected by the prime minister—in consultation with the appropriate church bodies. But his role as spiritual head of the Anglican Communion is taken into account at the time of his selection.

It is important to see the role of the archbishop of Canterbury properly as spiritual, but not administrative head of the Anglican Communion. He is no pope. He does not proclaim church doctrine, nor does he hold responsibility for, or wield authority over, the hierarchies of the Anglican churches worldwide. But with regard to the common fellowship of the communion, he does have practical functions—namely, to organize and preside over the Lambeth Conferences, as well as meetings of the primates of all the Anglican churches and of the Anglican Consultative Council, whose secretary general he supervises. Recent archbishops of Canterbury have increasingly taken their special role in the Anglican Communion to heart. They have often traveled overseas, visiting individual dioceses, national synods and conventions, and regional councils to testify to the worldwide fellowship of the communion. In all these activities it is difficult to separate the symbolic from the functional.

The principal mode of inter-Anglican debate has long been the Lambeth Conferences. These meetings of Anglican bishops from all over the world were begun in 1867 by Archbishop Longley at the repeated urging of the Canadian bishops, among others. Held at roughly ten-year intervals—interrupted by the two world wars—the gathering has outgrown Lambeth Palace, the London home of the archbishop, and has met most recently at Canterbury cathedral and the nearby University of Kent. Indeed, the number of bishops attending the conference has grown from seventy-six in 1867 to 525 in 1988. The essential purpose is for the bishops to come together for prayer and counsel. To be sure, discussions mold opinions—reports of commissions are accepted or rejected, resolutions are voted up or down—but for the individual churches of the communion these are purely advisory, not mandatory.

Since 1971, the Anglican Communion has had a second mode of common counsel, namely the Anglican Consultative Council. Derived from earlier consultative bodies, the council meets every other year, and includes lay people, clergy, and bishops among its delegates. National churches of more than a million members name three representatives; those with more than two hundred and fifty thousand, two; and all others, one. The archbishop of Canterbury, president of the council, traditionally leads the first session of each meeting, at which the council elects its own chair. (In 1974, an American, Mrs. Harold C. Kellerman, a former professor of pastoral theology at Virginia Seminary, served as chair.) With representatives from all orders of the communion, laity and clergy as well as bishops, the council has a special role to play in furthering the unity of the communion. It would certainly not be practical to hold world-wide church congresses of all orders. It is also helpful that the council meets with more frequency than the Lambeth Conferences.

Also serving to bring the Anglican churches together between Lambeth Conferences are meetings of the primates of all the member churches. Such meetings began in November 1979 and have continued since at two- or three-year intervals. Although the primates' meeting does not have the historical, or as yet the practical, significance of the Lambeth Conferences, or even of the meetings of the Anglican Consultative Council, it does provide a convenient way for the primates to confer. Recent meetings were held in Kenya in 1983 and Toronto in 1986. One indicator of the increasing importance of the primates' meeting is the recent allocation of stalls in the chapel at Lambeth Palace to the individual primates, each stall to be marked with the crest of the primate's church.

Regional cooperation among the Anglican churches

is secured through on-going regional councils, such as
the Council of the Churches of East Asia, and occa-
sional regional congresses. Thus, a Latin-American Anglican Congress was held in Panama in 1987, bringing
together for the first time representatives of the twenty-
seven Portuguese- and Spanish-speaking dioceses of
South and Central America. Pan-Anglican groups with
special interests also come together for meetings. Thus,
Anglican Charismatics met together in Canterbury before the Lambeth Conference of 1988.

Besides its official bodies, the Anglican Communion
has sought other ways to bring together its member
churches. With the development of new independent
churches within the Communion, the missionary work
of the Western churches was becoming something of an
anachronism. Yet clearly churches could be expected to
aid one another in many ways. Accordingly, in 1963
Anglicans embarked on a program of Mutual Responsibility and Interdependence in the Body of Christ,
designed to replace the older missionary programs.
This program did not succeed in altering old ways of
thinking, however, and a decade later it gave way to a
Partners in Mission program, which, in turn, was replaced by Ventures in Mission. One flourishing outcome of these various projects has been the Companion
Diocese Plan. In it, dioceses in different parts of the
world exchange aid, and their members visit back and
forth for better understanding. Such exchanges began
in the 1950s and have grown rapidly since.

One reason for consultation among the Anglican
churches is the existence of differences among them.
The deliberations of the 1988 Lambeth Conference gave
a good idea of what some of those differences are.

Many of the current problems of the Anglican churches stem from the dichotomy we have already noted between the Western and the third-world churches. Such differences are in fact superimposed on traditional splits between high and low church parties, between Anglo-Catholics and Evangelicals, between sacramentalists and social activists. It is indeed something of a hallmark of Anglicanism that its members seem always on the verge of separating under the pressure of irreconcilable differences. But at the time of the 1988 Lambeth Conference the differences seemed especially acute and many observers doubted that the Anglican Communion would emerge intact.

Each of the two groups of churches—from "developed" and "undeveloped" countries—has its own agenda. The "developed" churches inhabit secular, affluent societies. One aim of churches in such societies is to bring individuals at the margins of society back into the fold. Many within the Western churches, therefore, seek to enhance the position of marginal groups— women, gays, racial minorities—by creating more central positions for them in the church. They are also occupied with revisionary theology and concern themselves with such matters as inclusive language for scripture and liturgy, which does not characterize God as a (white) male.

Churches in the "undeveloped" world find such concerns irrelevant or counterproductive to their efforts to bring Christianity to indigenous people troubled by drought, famine, civil wars, social upheaval, lack of education, and want of even the necessities of life. For them, God the Father is a far more appealing figure than God the creator. And the third-world Anglican, for whom the gospel story of the sacrifice and resurrection of Jesus represents a hope for the future, is appalled to learn that some of his fellow churchmen are less than certain of the divinity of Christ. As a bishop for Pakistan told the Lambeth Conference of 1988 with some astonishment, "I hear some people here [Anglican bishops all] do not believe in the bodily resurrection of Jesus Christ." He would have been more astonished to learn how few of his other beliefs some of his fellow bishops shared.

Most significant of the differences between the two groups, however, is their attitude toward the role of women in the church. The move for ordination of women has been especially strong in the Western churches—though even there it is divisive. To the Asian and African churches, in regions where a woman's social role is most rigidly predetermined, the ordination of women seems an abomination. This conflict came much to the fore in the 1988 Lambeth Conference.

At the conference, as described in Michael Marshall's *Church at the Crossroads*, the traditional role of women in the church was strongly affirmed, even as it was questioned. While bishops were meeting to decide the future course of the Anglican Communion—including its treatment of women—a separate program was being held for the bishops' wives, dealing with such topics as pottery and flower arranging. But at the same time, a number of women priests were official consultants to the conference. One of them, a black American from Los Angeles, made history as the first woman priest to address a Lambeth Conference. She spoke with fervor and received a standing ovation—"from half the audience," as one observer wryly noted. Western women were themselves sharply divided on the subject. The English Movement for the Ordination of Women held daily events near the conference, while Women Against the Ordination of Women handed out materials to the conference participants.

Opposition to ordination was especially strong among delegates from Muslim areas, where Islamic fundamentalism is on the rise. There the ordination of women is seen as one more mark of the degeneracy of the West, and Christianity in particular. One third-world bishop told the conference that the ordination of women was "satanic." But opposition also came from Western traditionalists and from ecumenists who emphasized the difficulties such ordinations placed in the way of eventual union with the Roman Catholic and Eastern Orthodox churches.

By Lambeth 1988, however, ordination of women was a fait accompli. There have been several thousand Anglican women priests ordained since the 1970s. But it was fear of the impending consecration of women bishops that threatened the Anglican Communion most strongly at the 1988 Lambeth Conference. That the historic episcopate should be "contaminated" by the consecration of women seemed unthinkable to its opponents. Indeed many of them believed that priestly ordinations at which women bishops officiated and future episcopal consecrations in which they joined, would be invalid.

Yet, it was precisely toward such consecrations that the American church, among others, was moving. After much discussion, the conference failed to pass a resolution urging the member churches to refrain from consecrating women bishops. (It received 40 percent of the votes.) Instead the delegates strongly supported a resolution which left the matter in the hands of the individual churches, and requested the archbishop of Canterbury to appoint a commission to consult with each church in the aftermath of such consecration.

Certain bishops from the West—notably American bishops Spong and Moore—sought toleration for gays and others living together outside a typical marriage relationship, a situation increasingly common in Western societies. But the third-world bishops were not sympathetic. They insisted that all such relations were to be considered sinful, that all sexual relations outside of marriage were to be condemned. Even a resolution on AIDS was amended to avoid any appearance of condoning alternate life styles. As one African bishop said, "To support people who continue in sin, and to help them only not to be infected with the disease AIDS, that is not the gospel of Jesus Christ."

Yet the African bishops had their alternate life style for which they wished to secure approval from the conference. In certain African societies polygamy is the cultural norm, and African polygamists are reluctant to convert to Christianity if they are also expected to abandon their traditional way of life. Hence, African bishops sought approval for the baptism of polygamists, together with their multiple wives and offspring. Somewhat surprisingly perhaps, the assembled Anglican bishops went along with the request, in effect approving the polygamous marriages.

The third-world bishops scored another victory at the conference. Just as Anglicans generally oppose wars, so it could be supposed that they would be appalled by terrorism in all forms—especially considering the position of their own Terry Waite in the Middle East.

Nevertheless, the African bishops, led by Archbishop Desmond Tutu, were determined to win approval from the conference for those who, "after exhausting all other ways, use the way of armed struggle as the only way to justice." What they had in mind was the activities of the African National Congress against the South African government, which they wished Anglicanism as a body to endorse.

When the conference obliged and passed the resolution, apparently condoning terrorism everywhere in the world, the English public, which had recently suffered repeated bombings by the Irish Republican Army, was outraged. Somewhat surprised by the reaction, the bishops hastily drafted another resolution implying that while they had endorsed terrorism, they had not meant to include Irish terrorism. The terrorist captors of Terry Waite must have been much perplexed—or amused.

But it would be unfair to judge the Lambeth Conference of 1988 by its few aberrations. The Lambeth Conference had many successes. First, it resolved to reinforce the fourfold agencies of unity within the communion—the position of the archbishop of Canterbury, the primates' meeting, the Anglican Consultative Council, and the Lambeth Conferences. New ad hoc bodies were established, including an advisory body on prayerbooks to maintain a degree of commonality in the increasingly diverse liturgical practices of the churches.

Further, the conference moved to maintain traditional Anglican emphases on evangelism, ecumenism,
and social welfare. The call for Evangelical renewal was
strong, and among the resolutions was one proclaiming
a "Decade of Evangelism" in "the closing years of this
millennium." At the same time, the conference ad-
dressed social issues, directing attention (with perhaps
some clumsiness) toward AIDS and new social practices. Lambeth 1988 also reinforced the Anglican
churches' moves toward ecumenism. In all, it considered and endorsed fifteen ecumenical resolutions supporting continued dialogue with Lutherans, Roman
Catholics, and others. One of these called for interfaith
dialogues among Jews, Christians, and Muslims.

Above all, the conference once more affirmed the
continuing fellowship of Anglicans. A special feature
of the conference was the division of the bishops into
small groups, with members of diverse background, for
daily Bible study. According to one of the participants,
this practice brought them together in "love and respect" and reinforced their sense of "what it means to
be a member of the Anglican Communion." The
bishops talked together, prayed together, and celebrated the Eucharist together—the last so enthusi-
astically that more people were needed to administer
Communion at the daily Eucharist than planners had
allowed for.

Even such a vexed matter as the ordination of women
did not rupture the Anglican fellowship at Lambeth.
And in its resolution on the consecration of women
bishops, the conference may have set in place a mecha-
nism for ensuring that the continuing dispute would
remain only that. The conference spoke of the matter in
terms of "reception"—the reception by the worldwide

fellowship of the church of the actions of the individual member churches. Thus, the growing numbers of women Anglican priests were finding grudging but increasingly favorable reception within the various churches. If it was the will of the Holy Spirit that the church as a whole should come to accept women bishops, many Anglicans felt, the first consecration of such bishops would serve the purpose, however slowly, of opening the door to their more general acceptance, their more favorable reception by the whole body of the church.

For Anglicans, the future, no less than the present and the past, is fraught with hazards and filled with hopes. Some of the hazards we have seen—conflicts between churches in the "developed" and "undeveloped" worlds, disputes over the role of women in the church, differences over liturgical language and practice. But in one respect at least, these hazards are themselves hopes, for as Anglicans patiently, and with some forbearance, wrestle with their own differences, they are thrashing out the very problems that distress and divide the member churches of the larger Christian community.

In effect, the Anglican Communion, with its comprehensive character, is a microcosm of the macrocosm of Christianity as a whole. Its member churches of both East and West, its character both Catholic and Protestant, its concerns both sacramental and social, partake of much of the diverse nature of Christendom. It is, of course, especially for this reason that the Anglican churches feel themselves called so strongly to ecumenism. For many in the Anglican churches, the ordination of women seems a particular obstacle to ecumenism because of the determined opposition of Roman Catholics and the Eastern Orthodox churches. But those churches have their own women's movements. And among Protestant churches, Lutherans, Methodists, Presbyterians, Baptists, and others, now also have clergywomen. In this respect, too, the Anglican Communion is an ecclesiastical bridge, with some of its member churches ordaining women and some not. The Anglican experience of agonizing over this issue may ultimately make the Anglican churches more suitable merger partners for other churches which have had difficulty defining gender roles for their own members.

Above all, it is the Anglican experience of being many churches in one that holds a larger hope for the future. Anglicans are used to shared fellowship, and to communicating with those with whom they differ. It is their hope to continue that loving, and tolerating, association among themselves in the future. And ultimately, to include in it all their fellow Christians—indeed all their fellow believers in God.

Related Readings

THE BEST SHORT GENERAL INTRODUCTION TO THE EPISCO-
pal church is a paperback book, *The Episcopal Church
Welcomes You* (New York: Seabury Press, revised edition, 1979). This informative little book is by William
and Betty Gray. Another small paperback that gives
general background about the church is *Our Anglican
Heritage* (Elgin, Ill.: David C. Cook, 1977) by John W.
Howe. *Why I Am an Episcopalian* (Boston: Beacon
Press, 1965) is a moving account by one Episcopal
priest (now bishop), John McGill Krumm, of his voca-
tion. There is a good paperback history of the Church of
England, *Anglicanism* (Baltimore: Penguin, 1965) by
Stephen Neill.

Among the many other histories of the English
church are *The Anglican Tradition in the Life of England* by A. T. P. Williams (London: SCM Press, 1947)
and *Anglicanism in History and Today* by J. W. C.
Wand (London: Weidenfeld and Nicolson, 1961). An
excellent account of the more recent history of the
church is Canon Paul A. Welsby's *A History of the
Church of England, 1945–1980* (Oxford: Oxford University Press, 1984). For a scholarly analysis of the
present church from the perspective of political sci-

ence, the reader should see *Church and Politics in a Secular Age* (Oxford: Oxford University Press, 1988) by Kenneth Medhurst and George Moyser. The pros and cons of an establishment church are presented in Peter Cornwell's *Church and Nation* (Oxford: Basil Blackwell, 1983), while C. H. Sisson's *Anglican Essays* (Manchester: Carcanet Press, 1983) give one disaffected Anglican's reactions to the recent changes in the church.

An account of the state of the Anglican Communion today, focusing on a lively report of the Lambeth Conference of 1988, is given in Michael Marshall's *Church at the Crossroads* (San Francisco: Harper & Row, 1988). A more systematic analysis of Anglicanism in all its aspects is presented as *The Study of Anglicanism* (Philadelphia: SPCK/Fortress Press, 1988), edited by Professors Stephen Sykes and John Booty.

Raymond W. Albright's *A History of the Protestant Episcopal Church* (New York: Macmillan, 1964) is a comprehensive, detailed account of the formation, growth, and development of the Episcopal church. For the latest facts and figures on the church, the reader should consult the most recent edition of *The Episcopal Church Annual* (Wilton, Conn.: Morehouse-Barlow).

Two rather different views of the founding of the Episcopal church are contained in *Mitre and Sceptre* by Carl Bridenbaugh (New York: Oxford University Press, 1962) and *Bishops by Ballot* by Frederick V. Mills, Sr. (New York: Oxford University Press, 1978). William Wilson Manross's *The Episcopal Church in the United States 1800–1840* (1938; New York: AMS Press, 1967) is a study of the early years of the church. It is especially good at giving a sense of the life of the church at that time. A detailed study of the high church movement led by Bishop John Henry Hobart in those years is *Episcopal Vision/American Reality* (New Haven: Yale, 1986) by Robert Bruce Mullin.

Some of the recent changes in the Episcopal church are discussed in *Realities and Visions* (New York: Seabury Press, 1976), edited by Bishop Furman C. Stough and Professor Urban T. Holmes III. The new prayerbook is described and defended in Barry H. Evans's *Prayerbook Renewal* (New York: Seabury, 1978). An excellent review of recent events in the church is given in *The Episcopal Church in Crisis* (Cambridge, Mass.: Cowley Publications, 1988) by Professor John Booty.

Two very personal views of the events leading to the changes in the priesthood are the Rev. Carter Heyward's *A Priest Forever* (New York: Harper & Row, 1976) and *Take a Bishop Like Me* by Bishop Paul Moore, Jr. (New York: Harper & Row, 1979). Finally, detailed accounts of the new Pentecostal and Evangelical movements extending across church lines are given in two books by Richard Quebedeaux, *The New Charismatics* (Garden City, N.Y.: Doubleday, 1976) and *The Worldly Evangelicals* (New York: Harper and Row, 1978).

Index

byterians; Puritans
Puritans, 13-15, 17, 53-
54, 57, 58-59, 60; *see
also* Dissenters

Roman Catholic Church,
7, 9-10, 11, 12, 16, 24,
35, 36, 44, 49, 50, 96,
126, 144
Roman Catholics, 14-15,
19, 22, 24, 26, 55, 60,
74, 118, 119, 136, 155

Seabury, Samuel, 27, 64,
65, 67, 107
socialism, 82-83, 87
Society for the Propaga-
tion of the Gospel
(SPG), 56, 58, 59, 60,
61
Spong (Bishop), 97-98

Thirty-Nine Articles, 11,
14, 26, 123-124
Tractarians, 23, 73-74
Tutu, Desmond, 136, 152
Victoria (Queen), 25-26

Waite, Terry, 136, 152
Wesley, John, 20, 56, 61
Whitefield, George, 56-
57, 61
White, William, 64-65,
66, 67, 107
William and Mary, 16-
17, 26
Williams, Roger, 57, 60
William the Conqueror,
5, 6
World Council of
Churches, 35, 49, 90,
104
World War II, 32, 86, 88